FREUD FOR THOUGHT

FREUD FOR THOUGHT

ON FORGING
THE PHILOSOPHICAL LIFE

by Tom Donovan

Algora Publishing
New York

Library of Congress Cataloging-in-Publication Data —

Names: Donovan, Tom, 1967- author.
Title: Freud for thought : on forging the philosophical life / Tom Donovan.

Description: New York : Algora Publishing, [2023] | Includes
    bibliographical references and index. | Summary: "Prof. Tom Donovan
    suggests reading Freud today for aid in thinking about the human
    condition and inspiration to seize one's life. Philosophy can connect us
    to ourselves, our world, and our best traditions while training us in
    excellence and usefulness, blocking out some of the ridiculous things
    littering the contemporary world"— Provided by publisher.
Identifiers: LCCN 2023030956 (print) | LCCN 2023030957 (ebook) | ISBN
    9781628945188 (trade paperback) | ISBN 9781628945195 (hardcover) | ISBN
    9781628945201 (pdf)
Subjects: LCSH: Psychology—Philosophy. | Psychoanalysis. | Self. | Freud,
    Sigmund, 1856-1939.
Classification: LCC BF38 .D65 2023 (print) | LCC BF38 (ebook) | DDC
    150.1—dc23/eng/20230706
LC record available at https://lccn.loc.gov/2023030956
LC ebook record available at https://lccn.loc.gov/2023030957

Printed in the United States

For my dad, Tom Donovan Jr.
(1936–2022)

TABLE OF CONTENTS

Preface

When the NBA put basketball in the bubble in 2020 it showed that humans can pursue and achieve excellence even in, and perhaps partly through, adverse life circumstances. Around the same time, I reread Freud's *Civilization and its Discontents* and was pleasantly surprised with its enduring insights on the human condition. It addresses issues and ideas that provoke deeper philosophical thought. Freud's work connects us to the noble tradition of philosophy, going back to before Plato. Basketball and philosophy work the body and mind, and they can help us evolve and forge ourselves into higher beings. Adding a Freudian schema[1] onto these practices not only proves that Freud as philosopher is still relevant today but also delivers pleasure, self-knowledge, and tools for building a good community. It shows us the path to true happiness.

Freud is best read today for aiding us in thinking about the human condition and, despite his pessimistic view of our nature, as inspiration to seize one's life. Freud does for philosophical theory what basketball can do as athletic practice. They connect us to ourselves, our world, and our best traditions. They strengthen our minds and bodies. All this is part of living *la vie philosophique*. A philosophical way of living teaches us to reflect on our individual lives, the community, and the highest aspects of what it means to be human. Further, it puts us in contact with the true meaning of our quotidian lives. Together philosophy, Freud, and basketball can train us in noble

---

[1] The chapters in this book follow the chapters in Freud's *Civilization and its Discontents* to offer a philosophical reading of some of its themes, while often utilizing basketball as analogue.

comportment, excellence, and usefulness, while at the same time helping to block out some of the ridiculous things littering our contemporary world.

I owe a profound debt to Christine Duvergé for reading and editing the complete manuscript, as well as for all the splendid conversations surrounding this book. Thanks to Mt. San Jacinto College for granting my sabbatical during spring semester 2023. Thank you to Algora Publishing for continuing to support my writing, and especially to Andrea and Martin for their care and excellence throughout every step of the publishing process.

CHAPTER 1 — GREAT INTUITIONS

> It is impossible to escape the impression that people commonly
> use false standards of measurement—that they seek power, success
> and wealth for themselves and admire them in others, and that they
> underestimate what is of true value in life.[2] — Sigmund Freud

At this point in history, couldn't we be striving to live according to "what
is of true value in life"? Shouldn't we measure our lives by true standards?[3]
We all know that the pursuit of power, success, and wealth do not lead
to true happiness. They do not make life meaningful. They do not give us
knowledge of ourselves. Still, we are rather attracted to them. Why? We
insist on pursuing them. Why? We often ignore what we know is important.
Why? These are some of the fundamental questions Freud seeks to answer.

More or less, we all intuitively understand the meaning of life, and we all
know that we should not get sidetracked or squander our short existence
on this planet. We repeat to each other, and ourselves, clichés such as "life's
too short" and "you only live once." Giving in to the worst instincts within
ourselves or placating them in others makes no one proud. Despite the temptation and prevalence of superficial lives, Freud points out that, nonetheless,
most of us have no problem admitting we should strive for better things.
We do tend to admire those who take up the difficult but good fight of a
higher and serious life. We see that there's a type of greatness in not letting
celebrity culture and contemporary materialism dictate one's hopes and
desires. We know that material objects and social labels don't make for indi-

---

[2] Sigmund Freud, *Civilization and its Discontents* (Norton Press, 2010), p. 23.
[3] Freud's articulations such as "true value in life" and "false standards of measurement" are
ontologically and epistemologically suspect. Yet, it should become clear why it's appropriate to mimic Freud's language.

---

vidual happiness or freedom. We recognize, even if we can't always fight against it ourselves, that pursuing power, success, and wealth are not the roads to true meaning, deep happiness, or self-knowledge. We understand that vulgar pursuits can corrupt us to the depths of our souls, as a manner of speaking. We know that vice breeds vice. We are smart even when we are not living smartly. Yet are we too modern to pursue what's truly good? Are we too clever to pursue excellence and greatness? Are we too cool to have noble comportment? We certainly understand that we are complicated beings who will not always get ourselves to do what we know is best or highest. Sometimes, though, we even convince ourselves that shallow things are important. Or, perhaps, others are convincing us as Plato suggested with his allegory of the cave.

Plato advocated for excellence and thought that it took a certain birth luck (that he was willing to rig) and a serious bit of training. Still, to live by a true standard does not require that one do something great. Plato thought that everyone has skills and qualities that are useful, and everyone can pursue excellence. Through these, we come to know ourselves and our role in the community. When we are being useful and pursuing excellence we can make sense of our lives and connect that sense to others. This makes life meaningful and worth living. Living a life valuing the correct things is great in itself and allows us to experience real, concrete fulfillment. Further, when we achieve these, material success and fame become uninteresting. For we can have material wealth, be idolized, and still not achieve excellence, be useful, self-knowing, moral, or noble. While both Freud,[4] and certainly Plato,[5] valued those who are highly capable and willing to achieve greatness, we do not need to follow them in this. Noble today should mean valuing everyone who is being useful and pursuing excellence. But, still, let's look at *greatness* a little more carefully.

On Greatness

One can be great at something and still not be great. And no matter how great one becomes at one or two things, no one will be great at everything. But does it then follow that one cannot live a great life? We need to be careful

---

[4] Freud begins *Civilization and its Discontents* praising his friend for his greatness. He then promptly demolishes his friend's metaphysical claims, and as such, gives us an instance of affirming and prioritizing true standards.

[5] At the same time, Plato expected more from the guardians and rulers, including that they put themselves more at risk of dying and that they sacrifice part of their life for the common good. Those he valued the most were required to give up the most. Those who are higher and have developed themselves have more to give.

and not get seduced into thinking that it is *sufficient* to be great, as in among the best at something, to live a worthwhile life. For instance, an intellectual who is a great intellectual but is a crummy and miserable person or a money making entrepreneur who treats the employees poorly. Their success was not enough to make their lives noble. Further, we need to avoid the bait that it is *necessary* to be great at something to pursue excellence in life, as in those who don't do anything explicitly extraordinary but are useful and virtuous. These people carry themselves well in almost all contexts. They understand how to act in varying environments. When we develop these qualities, our individual selves evolve and become more coherent over time. As such, you are not so rigid that you cannot adapt when necessary, and you are not so fluctuating that one cannot trace a coherent self through the varying situations and stages of your life. That's an important part of the art of living: developing and utilizing one's capabilities and qualities without congealing one's individuality or dissolving one's duties. As the French put it: *C'est en forgeant qu'on devient forgeron.*

C'est en forgeant qu'on devient forgeron is often translated as "practice makes perfect." The French approach however is not abstract, naive, or essentialist. It's by working with a forge that one becomes a blacksmith. It's concrete, contextual, and emphasizes actual labor, directed toward a noble pursuit. There's nothing perfect about any of it. No one lives a perfect life and it's a misunderstanding of the human condition to aim for perfection. Aiming for perfection is an imperfection and sometimes a ploy to avoid living by true or virtuous standards. Rather than working hard to better oneself, to evolve, it's a retreat into magical thinking, which often is just a symptom of an essentialist desire or a Nietzschean will to power. Human life is a constant becoming and is only coherent with reality when seen within a perspective of movement, growth, and overcoming. If I were perfect I could not become what I already was. If I was imperfect I couldn't become perfect, as no one's past can be completely erased. Something perfect cannot become more perfect, but something imperfect can strive and become excellent. Wanting perfection is like trying to be young again. Nostalgia can be a trap. One must guard against non-mature impulses, especially those that create a fantasy of the past as well as those that invent a make-believe future. Temptations to essentialize and, according to Freud, the impulse to remain childlike, are among the biggest hurdles to overcome if one wants to live in accordance with true standards. We must be in tune with the contexts that we find ourselves actually living in rather than turning toward fantasies, ideas, and running from our existence. Immaculate desires seduce us away from contemplating the dirty truth that "we are born between urine and feces."[6] Freud's image is to remind us of what we are and signals that he doesn't expect much from most people. Still, let's also be sure not to expect too little from creatures born, in many cases, from love between two people.

Whether or not the ideal biological and societal conditions are present to start one's life, the quest for greatness is a difficult one. Only some of us will achieve greatness in anything. There's a ton of basketball players on the planet but not a lot of great ones. And some that are not great also are not great at anything else. Yet they can pursue excellence by taking their pursuits seriously and putting care into what they do, and by refusing false standards and pursuing true ones. Conversely, those achieving something great in some sphere or another may, nevertheless, pursue false standards of measurement in their life, and hence, their achievements won't grow them into useful or virtuous people. Others, who may not achieve what we label as greatness, might still live according to truth, be useful, take life seriously, and internalize the ideals that match what is best in our species. This makes one noble. The sense of nobility we are following here finds its roots in the French *noble*, meaning: knowable, distinguished, splendid, and excellent. We should not interpret being noble as a class value. Rather, it's a higher human value that connects each of us with what is most splendid in our character and in our species. It signals that you are worthy of respect, are knowable and brilliant in yourself, and that you have lofty qualities, especially moral ones. Freud understands that infants start out as little savages that must evolve into full human beings. We are, at our beginning, potentially "noble savages." When we are young, we are wild beasts, yet the seeds of our greater capabilities and qualities are starting to sprout. To grow with beauty, we must take root, digest the proper nourishment, and elevate out of the dirt. Living a truly meaningful life requires knowledge of the self and of the human condition. Declining the false standards to actualize the true ones is indispensable and proves to be more difficult than trying to be great at something, especially in a society obsessed with celebrity and materialist standards.

What is the origin of the false standards? There are many causes and they run deep, but let's begin with where we are today. We live in a modern capitalist society. Simply put, money drives most things in our world today. We are seduced constantly by the schema of money,[7] either directly or indirectly. We are pressured to pursue it, we succumb to the values it pushes. True, we must have money to survive in our world. Thus, in some contexts it's rational to seek it, while in others it's not. Still it's difficult and complicated,

---

[6] *Civilization and its Discontents*, p. 88.
[7] Christian Lotz, *The Capitalist Schema* (Lexington, 2016).

because even when we know we shouldn't care too much about what others are doing or saying, we recognize that we cannot completely not care. After all, we are social creatures that must compare and contrast our lives with others to even know what is going on in reality. That being the case, capitalism or not, we will be impacted both psychologically and physically if we reject the dominant schema of our society. In any social environment, human beings will probably struggle to stay on point when it comes to pursuing what is of true value in life, unless the social structure and socialization are designed to encourage us and reward us for living according to it. Yet it's not clear that any society can or really would want to do that. Societies aim to perpetuate themselves, and they want stability. They don't really care if we find our lives deep and meaningful. Clearly, capitalism is not designed for this value, but rather it is designed to encourage and reward market capabilities and consumer desires.

Still, capitalism doesn't seem especially problematic when you compare it to other actual existing economic systems. If it is true that we are social creatures who cannot avoid comparing our lives to others, then seeking wealth, success, and power perhaps cannot be completely avoided. After all, every and all societies value them to some degree. Chasing, let's call them capitalist-type goods, might not be the underlying cause of underestimating what is of true value in life, but rather it might simply be an obstacle to what a social being is up against when trying to live by a true standard. To limit the power of society's dominant norms, one might first have to see that they are not good for one as an individual. The pursuit of individual happiness and excellence, that interests Freud, is not a surface quest. This sort of excellence stems from the etymology of the Latin *excellentia*, meaning surpassing, being superior, and rising out of oneself. This way of getting out of oneself is through evolving and working from within the history of the self. Freud understood that the self has layers, and simply scratching at the surface will not allow one to go deep into the self. The French speak of *la nature profonde* as our true nature. The adjective *profonde*, as in deep, is important here. It's a nature that must be actualized through work. Nietzsche affirms this vision in showing us that to become who we are is to know our nature and create it. It's not something stagnant, rather it's *la nature profonde*. We can think of it as deep sea diving: heavy work, lacking oxygen, scary but also very calm, soundless, in search of buried treasures. It's impossible for me to achieve this feeling if I am attached to social labels, commodities, or if I have mistaken another's life and success for my own. Most social standards, and materialistic goods and honors, are false, in that they distract me from growing my self into something splendid. To evolve, I must get into the deep of *my* existence, focus through the cloudy water, move in accordance with the waves, be present under the sea, and capture all that exists far below the buzzing, blooming world above.

This quest is rather different from the dominant quests that our society advocates. Contemporary society, at best, offers watered down versions of an evolutionary inspired *excellence. La vie philosophique* style of excellence stresses being useful, pursuing meaning in this world, and valuing one's deep individuality and true freedom. Living a philosophical life means rejecting values that hinge on popularity. Our philosophical quest means one must have the strength to do what is right, especially when it requires having to go one's own way. Of course, it is tough to focus on the noble pursuits in life when one sees the advantages others seem to have when they do acquire wealth, success, and power. I might tell myself, then, that the problem of them being false has only to do with making them central to my existence, or pursuing these things at the expense of something greater. For some people seem to have both the spoils of life and are living a noble existence. If this is the case, I can make the argument that seeking capitalist-type goods in the name of helping me live a meaningful and useful life is rational. Still, I must be wary: chasing capitalist values is exhausting without the guarantee that I will catch them. I might, however, miss out on living a true and deeper life because I got distracted aiming for superficial goods.

Nevertheless, humans are complex and even if we don't aim for the higher good that Freud praises, we will probably admire those who seek it and, like Freud, we probably have no trouble calling these men and women "great" for having the courage, attributes, and possibly luck, to pursue a higher calling and achieve it, while renouncing more direct pleasures and popularity. For example, we would probably appreciate and praise a heart surgeon willing to get up early and work hard every day doing heart surgeries to save lives. This is surely not as directly pleasurable and fun as hosting a television show and having housewives gushing over you. Further, one probably makes more money doing the latter, especially if one is willing to promote dubious products. Therein lies an interesting aspect of human complexity: most of us realize that a life of celebrity is shallow and insipid, but we also realize that it would be hard to turn such a life down if the opportunity for it arose. *Quelle horreur!*

There are many layers, for just as we can understand people who achieve even when we recognize that their achievements are not helping humanity, we can respect those who do seek to make the world better or devote their life to some cause, even if we would never consider doing such a thing. Or, maybe, we realize we couldn't do such a thing. There's no shame in saying "I could never achieve like Einstein." We can also admire those who don't want any sort of social or intellectual greatness. There is something deeply noble about not striving to do anything world-changing, and simply focusing our energy on being useful to those we care about and have duties to. That should count for much. Isn't it a type of greatness? Aiming to be useful within one's immediate, concrete, quotidian world is a beautiful thing. At the same time, we can contrast this with, and be skeptical of, those self-proclaimed saviors of humanity that Emerson warned us about and who seem to be driving today's actual existing "justice" projects.

Besides the chore of distinguishing types of greatness and separating out the great from the pretend great, we should mention the spoils that may accompany certain success. When some people achieve a certain type of greatness they may think this entitles them to other desserts and advantages. Frequently, it's not just the people who achieve something great that try to get more, it's often those around them who try to give them more. It seems to be part of human nature that we turn those who achieve greatness into idols. This is dangerous as the move from admiration to idolization makes one infantile. Still, we recognize that it's hard not to want to be close to greatness and it's easy to over-reward greatness. Thus, it might be rational to grant a certain authority to those who achieve greatness. The very fact of achieving greatness in something means that you have literally done something better than most others. Perhaps you have trouble explaining it or teaching it, but the fact that you actually achieved something seems relevant and makes you an authority. Plenty of people are great talkers but many who achieve are not. Their authority comes from action, from direct material reality, and this is a space in which words do not dominate. Words only have power so long as people are listening. They require others to buy what one is selling. Just saying one is great is not great. Great actions may speak for themselves. Great actions create beyond words and above mere ideas; we should grant actual greatness its authority.

Of course, it is fallacious to grant someone authority in something he or she is not really an authority in. It's so common though that we had to give it a name in philosophy. It's not a clever name: "appeal to unqualified authority," but it makes the point that we must logically connect authority to something. It's rational and smart to appeal to an authority about something in which the person is an authority. If you have training, education, experience, or have shown excellence in something, then it makes sense to defer to you. Appealing to an authority is not fallacious in itself. Rather, it's fallacious when we appeal to an unjustified authority. To avoid the fallacy we must appeal to the relevant authority within each context, for being an expert in one thing does not make one an expert in another. Being great in one thing does not mean one will be great at other things or that one will be noble.

Is one who lives a great life an authority on living a great life? What does it even mean to live a great life? Certainly, a useful life has certain advantages over just doing something great. We might think that everyone is an authority on his or her own life, but it's not true. Many people play basketball, but many don't do so with excellence or really understand the game. An authority on living a noble human life requires living life by pursuing excellence and cultivating one's skills and qualities in useful activities. When this happens, you move yourself into truly meaningful environments, and real human trust can develop. Human connections towards oneself and with others take form. Higher creations happen. We see the beauty of it, for instance, when The Golden State Warriors were winning multiple championships. Even if they were the nemesis to our team, we couldn't help but admire the supreme way they played. If they were playing against our team, even if our team was winning, we feared and expected trouble in the third quarter. We all saw that the Warriors had another level of greatness, and there was nothing anyone could do to stop it. In effect, they were the justified authority of the NBA with their sage-like presence on the court. In the context of a human life we call some people sages when we see they are thriving in the same sort of way.

Sages are rare. We should be wary of thinking our authority is unquestionable. For even a qualified authority will miss certain things. Those on the inside are not infallible. The marginalized or outside perspective can be enlightening and provide needed perspective. Thus, even when we grant authorities their authority, we don't have to trust them blindly. We can take the time to check that what they are saying or doing is consistent with reason and reality. We can check to see if their competence matches their title. Simply calling someone "doctor" doesn't make that person great, an authority, or excellent at his or her craft. A qualified authority should be able, at some level, to explain or show concretely what he or she is an authority on.

Being on the outside does give a different perspective, yet we have to be careful with fetishizing the outside or the marginalized perspectives. Humans have the tendency to overestimate their insight when they are on the outside. They don't see, perhaps literally, all that is going on, but often think they do. This is apparent when people are watching a sport they are unfamiliar with. They will often ask questions or make observations that are off point or not interesting. They just don't know what's going on yet, and might need to grow themselves, and show patience and modesty, to be worthy of understanding and participating in that environment. Some things cannot be seen immediately and time is necessary for knowledge and true understanding. Both those on the inside and those on the outside need to listen as much as they speak. As far back as at least the 4th century BCE, Pythagoras and other philosophers emphasized the value of listening. We have to train ourselves to listen. Those coming from a position of power need to ensure they are hearing the outside voices and should seek to understand and incorporate the rational and relevant ones. Further, those on the outside need to be patient and try to understand the logic of the tradition until they get into the swim of the practice. Dialogue is an art. We have to train ourselves to speak to each other and not just roar. Modesty and an enlightened view on tradition, to play with a Gadamerian[8] phrase, does a lot of work when it comes to understanding the true measurement of things. Still, the hermeneutics of all this gets complicated and there are many ways to get it wrong. Getting it right is part of the art of living, and it's worth the physical and dialogical effort. For speaking and listening to each other, acting individually and collectively, while aiming for truth and understanding, is all we have if the goal is living by true standards. That's a lot, and it's easy to get off point in many spheres of life.

In sports, it's harder to get sidetracked. That's one of the things that makes sports so great. The environment almost forces one to be focused. True focus is the ability to be in the present moment in the relevant way, to concentrate only on what matters. In a basketball game, what matters is how well one plays. It's not helpful to be reflecting on what's going on somewhere else in the world or what I believe about any other issue or even about what is the meaning of my opponent's red hat. It's about zoning in on the speed and flow of the game, on whether the other players are right or left handed, where they shoot well, how to lock them down on defense, etc. This comportment gives us a concrete model for staying on point and striving for excellence. A professor teaching Plato ought to teach Plato in the classroom, just like the basketball player ought to play basketball while on the court. In both cases, for success, one needs to be good at the activity and in touch with the relevant qualities of others in that environment. But in the classroom, where I'm in a position of power, it's easier to abuse and hence spoil the environment. I do this if I start playing a different game, such as going off on some tangential thought or irrelevant infatuation not connected to philosophy.

This propensity to veer off track is exacerbated in a Godless society, a society that has replaced God with Capitalism. Not only is it easier to drift, but one should ask the deeper question of what is the motivation of

---

[8] See Gadamer, *Truth and Method* (Continuum, 1989).

remaining on point. What does one gain for attempting to be higher, noble, virtuous, and good? What is the reward in our society? Is it worth the work if only endless death awaits us? This problem has been brewing for some time now. Many of Molière's[9] works explore this dilemma, and he captures the contradictions that arise in such structures. For example, those bourgeoisie who had the desire for elevation, those who wanted to elevate themselves by emulating the few noble who were actually noble, are ridiculed in a way that shows what's at stake, as well as the conditions and limitations of evolution. Today it's clear that in the modern social transvaluation of values we didn't extend, and perhaps couldn't have extended, our highest virtues throughout the classes of society. Rather, we might say, inauthenticity won; or to put it in Heideggerian jargon, a *das man* superficial fleeing of human anxiety won.[10] Nobility certainly did not win, and today it has a bad reputation. Further, those who only know how to roar remind us of this every day.

Sports such as basketball harbor noble values. They continue to give us deeper insight into excellence, usefulness, and evolution. At a game everyone has a role connected to the game, and when we all play our roles it's a successful event and a lovely thing to be part of. On the court, there might be only one or two great players, but everyone can be useful and pursue excellence. A college classroom and a basketball game are social situations that only work when we adhere to the relevant values, and if everyone plays their role responsibly. Trying to make the activity function at a high or noble level is a better way of thinking about it than asking "I am living my best life?" or "Am I being my true self?" These latter ways of thinking, besides their commodified essence, misunderstand the contextual, relational, and intersubjective nature of our lives. It's not really about the "I," as it's more complicated than that. This doesn't mean that trying to be one's best is wrong, but we should see it doesn't truly capture the concrete situation one is in. Athletes may speak in clichés when being interviewed, but while playing we can be sure that Nikola Jokić is not thinking about being his "true self."[11] Rather he is acting, largely pre-reflectively, to help his team win. His greatness comes from years of careful work, not from thinking about an identity. It's not about imagining that you have many selves and then trying to pick the best version for the big dance. We don't have various potential selves, ready-to-hand, lined up like clothes in a closet. Just like consumers are today

---

[9] See especially *Les Précieuses ridicules* (1659), *Le Bourgeois gentilhomme* (1670).

[10] See Heidegger, *Being and Time* (Harper, 1962), esp. Division I. ch. 27.

[11] Still, we are beginning to see the impact of the new ideology as younger players are internalizing it. Of course, the consequences for these individuals and for the game are depressing.

experiencing choice fatigue, we are confusing and distracting individuals with what we might call "self-choice fatigue."

Because of the media and culture industry's ability to get us to think in terms of products, many today have a present-at-hand ideological image of an essential self. The notion of an essential or true self, inside oneself, just waiting to come out is just a superstition. Our Manichean culture feeds and creates it because it's a money-maker. Black and white and black versus white is the cynical formula peddled today. It's a game of "them against us," "us against them," a game that leads nowhere close to excellence, virtue, and nobility. Modern society, after the death of God, cleansed itself of spirituality, and yet it still needs to fill the emptiness left by this loss. A world disenchanted threatens to become nothing but a wasteland, populated with manufactured needs sold to a confused populace willing to buy, in form, only two commodities. One is dystopia and the other utopia. It's a warfare strategy: shock and awe.[12] Nobility and the pursuit of excellence require rejecting all the empty calories of our mass society.

Still, the very fact that we strive beyond what we can see shows there's still hope. Many of us want a better world, a nobler life, and we need to make sense of our existence. Many of us don't have to brand and label everything, especially not ourselves. We understand that existence goes deeper than labels and we refuse to obsess over them. Our bodies sense the dangers, fragmentations, and emptiness threatening existence. Our physical selves signal to us the truth of human existence, and our mortal bodies capture the truth emanating from and through our lived existence. We are our existence. We know that the opposite of it is a nothingness. Contemporary society desensitizes us. It encourages us to be infantile. It gets hung up on words and misses the metaphysics of the deeper reality; a lived reality that escapes words as signs, and transcends the roaring that often accompanies shallow banter and vulgar barking. If words are truly important to us, we should trace their etymology and aim to keep the living meaning of them alive. We should not reduce our lived language to the beeps of advertising jingles or the random associations of the ignorant. It's not a conspiracy theory to recognize that there are forces in the modern world that are manipulative and unhealthy. We have the right to reject them. When we do, we deny their power. We seize our individuality and our human existence in situations that are real and relevant to our lives. Living this way will make our lives meaningful and virtuous even though it necessitates years of work. Excellence is not a bargain. The life of philosophy must be chosen.

---

[12] Georg Lukács, *Writer and Critic* (Merlin, 1978). See esp. the preface where he refers to it as "shock and manipulated alienation."

Our focus on contexts and situations might prompt the question: If greatness is dependent on specific contexts, can we coherently say anything about greatness above and beyond each various context? Can we speak of Greatness with a capital "G," so to speak? Can we coherently consider trans-contextual greatness? If every context or situation is different, how can we compare them, let alone try to add them up into something more? In other words, can we coherently say someone *is Great*, or do we have to specify the context? If it's the latter, do we have to distinguish higher from lower contexts? How do we rank contexts? Do we have to analyze the context, and if the activity of one is greater than another, are we forced to conclude that the person who achieves greatness in the greater activity is greater than the one who achieves greatness in the lesser activity? What about the person who achieves only semi-greatness in the higher context versus someone who achieves super-greatness in a lower context? *C'est beaucoup de questions, non?*

Without an external standard to rank what counts as greatness, we might be forced to say that both Einstein and Lebron are great in each respective context, and that's it. Lebron is great when we are talking about basketball and Einstein is great when we are thinking about physics. Can we say that Lebron lives his life by a false standard and Einstein did not? I'm sure you see how tricky it can be to determine. Freud is interested in civilization, so we might be tempted to say Einstein's life follows a truer and higher path since his advances in physics are more useful for civilization. Are they really? If they aid in the ability to make weapons of mass destruction and civilization ends, then what? Or, conversely, if Lebron, as part of an entertainment industry, which basketball is now driven by, keeps our anti-civilizing tendencies at bay, then is basketball more beneficial or greater than theoretical physics? This is confusing. Still, we can point out that no one can transcend his or her particular life or the human condition. Yet we can evolve as individuals, and, perhaps, as a species. As such, the more virtuous contexts we become useful in, the deeper we strive for excellence, and the more nobility we carry ourselves with, the more meaningful, splendid, and great our lives will become. If Lebron is crummy and miserable in his life off the court, then he is great at something but that's it. And the same for Einstein.

Should we conclude that "Greatness" with a capital G is a myth, a childish fantasy that ties itself to the idea of perfection? Probably. It is diffi-cult to speak in absolutist terms and general labels without jumping to a metaphysical belief or some sort of external standard. If we have a religious foundation, then, perhaps, we can unambiguously rank contexts and talk about greatness with a capital "G." Many athletes like to say: "God is Great!" Any specific situation or activity that gets one closer to God is greater than any profane activity. Further, to devote one's whole life to God is to live a great life. Going to heaven suggests that one's life was great. But what if we remove God from the puzzle? Are these moves possible or even desirable? Freud has profound answers to these questions. His suggestions for living consistent with *la nature profonde* are worth investigating. *La vie philosophique* aims to create lives of deep meaning and value. Living a philosophical life stresses the evolution of the individual and looks honestly at the potential and limits of any civilization. Although the focus is on evolution, the quest requires a backwards, as well as forward, analysis of the self.

The Ocean

That first paragraph about greatness, and true versus false standards of valuation in *Civilization and its Discontents*, may seem to be almost a throwaway paragraph in the sense that it is not directly what the book is about. Still, these issues shadow Freud's larger argument and have profound significance for philosophy and religion. In his compact book *Future of an Illusion*, Freud criticizes religion. One of his friends wished that he had discussed the awe that many religious people claim they experience: the feeling of something larger happening behind the scenes of life, a deep sense of connection with something somewhat unexplainable and vast as the true source of the religious sentiment. Freud calls this an "oceanic feeling." What exactly is the oceanic feeling? It's hard to say. "Oceanic feeling" is not a term we typically use in philosophy. We do speak of a "metaphysical urge" though, which may be described as a feeling but need not be. A metaphysical urge signals an urgency. In some, the urgency may be as strong as a *need*, while in others it is experienced merely as a *desire*. In either articulation, the metaphysical urge is the impulse to believe in something that transcends this world. In other words, it's a need or desire to connect to something higher than the finite human condition. In this sense, then, the metaphysical urge may initiate or come out of a feeling. One might experience the oceanic feeling and that prompts the belief in transcendence. Or, one might literally have a need to transcend human existence. From this need, I could motivate, within myself, an oceanic feeling. In short, a metaphysical urge could either originate from a feeling or simply be a wish for such a feeling. To illustrate: I may be hungry, and that hunger might make me believe in something greater. "I'm hungry, and there's food here, clearly the universe loves me, and we are one." Or I could be bored and develop an urge to eat. "There's nothing to do. I wish it were time for dinner!" A desire for it to be time to eat might actually make me feel hungry.

Freud explains that his friend "would like to call it a sensation of 'eternity', a feeling as of something limitless, unbounded—as it were, 'oceanic'."[13] Freud emphasizes the word "oceanic" in his analysis. This is clever, as it signals Freud's urge (need or desire?) to conceive of this sensation in human terms. Oceans are part of this world and we know they are not limitless or unbounded or eternal, but they often seem that way. Freud's friend calls the sensation "a purely subjective fact, not an article of faith; it brings with it no assurance of personal immortality, but it is the source of the religious energy."[14] Further, his friend claims that the awareness of this sensation alone renders the definition of a person as religious. One need not look to the external world or for divine inspiration or study any specific creed or dogma to find God. Proto-religious feelings are something basic and general; perhaps one might call these a feeling of awe that inspires or prompts a belief in the supernatural. Whatever we call it, the implication is that it is intuitive, immediate, and, for some, apparently, ever-present. It begins with a physical sensation, desire, idea, or need so moving or so powerful that one cannot deny that there is more going on than meets the eye. Further, it means one must conclude that there is a deep oneness underlying a world that appears differentiated, separate or even fragmented.

Two questions come immediately to mind: Does everyone experience the oceanic feeling, and do we also experience the opposite? The answer to the first is no, not everyone. At least Freud says he has never experienced it, and ask around and you will find many like Freud. It's not a universal experience in the sense that we usually speak of universals. For the second question, the answer is yes. Many people speak of feeling completely alone in the world, of having a deep feeling, urge, or perhaps even a need in them that all is fragmented and transient. Further, this sense may be accompanied with a sense of dread or a feeling that everything is falling apart, ending fast and too soon, and is irreparable. In some it is intuitive, immediate, ever-present, and nihilistic. As a feeling it can become an urge to ponder, and even cultivate disunity. Imagine an oceanic space all dried up after nuclear fallout, comparable to something out of a Tarkovsky film. A feeling of everything fractured, alienated, and limited everywhere. Can we call this the anti-metaphysical urge? Does everyone experience this? Could there also be an un-metaphysical urge?

Rather than simply playing with or dismissing a religiously interpreted oceanic feeling, it might be more fruitful, and greater, to try to work with it. After all, it's not a bad sensation, and although I like my space, I also,

---

[13] *Civilization and its Discontents*, p. 24.
[14] Ibid.

de temps en temps, enjoy the feeling of community and connection with other people, things, events, and perhaps nonevents. Further, we don't want to discourage ourselves from contemplating beyond what is visible. Our world is fragmented, and seeking to become whole can be a noble pursuit. Our world can become better, thus a holding to a certain flavor of utopian impulse is healthy. We must also embrace our individuality and the truth that our death ends the human condition for each of us. We live our lives in specific contexts but we sense our lives as a totality. Trying to get the parts to fit with the whole and the whole to fit with the parts is the route for capturing true meaning and knowledge. A hermeneutic or interpretive approach is consistent with Freudian analysis, despite his surface critique of the oceanic feeling as simply infantile residue. Freud understood the deep conflicts that will be present between an individual and others, the environ-ment, and even within the individual as a self. Yet he equally understood the desire, need, and possibilities stemming from a certain sort of oneness and harmony concerning it all. Freud's project warns us against unreflectively accepting either a metaphysical urge or an anti-metaphysical urge. Rather, we need to critically understand both urges, and then interpret them, so that we can build and rebuild ourselves into greatness. Living a philosophical life requires coming to terms with the varying urges that both prompt us to dive into a seemingly bottomless ocean, and at other times, just to sun ourselves on an isolated beach.

The metaphysical urge that seeks transcendence beyond the visible takes various forms. Freud began this discussion with the ocean feeling, yet today, we might more readily speak in terms of *faith* when pondering further than the "eye" can see. Freud's friend distinguishes the oceanic feeling from faith. He says that the oceanic feeling is "a purely subjective fact, not an article of faith."[15] Do we agree with this? Are the two connected? In a strict sense, the oceanic feeling is solely a feeling, while faith is a leap beyond any feeling. Faith is closer to a belief or a hope that something will happen, despite the facts, and regardless of any literal feeling. Faith can pitch itself against reason and can defy or challenge it, while the oceanic feeling, strictly interpreted, stands or falls on empirical grounds. Faith comes to the back door when knowledge is not at the front door. Faith might exist when one feels nothing. Yet faith is not present, when one has knowledge or clear understanding. When one has knowledge, one doesn't need faith. Faith is a sort of backup plan. Is faith an anti-knowledge feeling? None of this is straightforwardly or necessarily purely positive or negative. Of course, we should generally be led by knowledge and reason, yet some things are unknowable, and the world

---

[15] Ibid.

is not completely reasonable. Sometimes it's appropriate for us to be unreasonable. Some aspects of our lives cannot be captured simply through rationality, empiricism, or other traditional ways of understanding.

Still, some cannot tolerate faith or, perhaps, have no faith in faith. Faith just doesn't speak to some people. Some of us are moved by rationality or, we might say, wired up to look at the world logically. Does trying to understand everything through logic make us illogical? Can one be irrationally rational? The ancient philosopher Anaximander had strong logical intuitions that he applied to metaphysical thinking. Shortly after Thales concluded "everything is water," Anaximander countered with the idea of the "unbounded" or the "infinite." The unbounded, Anaximander stated, is what holds the four essential elements together. Different than a feeling, urge, or irrational belief though, it was articulated as a logical claim. The idea was that, logically speaking, something infinite must exist that transcends the four basic elements (earth, air, fire, water). This infinite "something" allows the basic elements to exist independently, as well as holding the world together as one. Anaximander's unbounded or infinite could be thought of as a type of faith. Still it would be faith in the necessity of logic. Anaximander's claim is a metaphysical one, as he attempts to push us beyond what we can immediately see. This urge to describe reality using deep logic connects to the oceanic feeling. But whereas the oceanic feeling presents itself as a subjective fact, the unbounded aims to be an *objective fact*. A logical fact that all rational individuals "see" as necessary to make sense of the universe, and, perhaps also their lives in it.

Freud stresses that we cannot just accept the various intuitions or metaphysical claims we have floating inside of us. He also knows most of us will have strong intuitions inside of us that we did not choose. Thus, we don't want to simply ignore them or attempt to quickly discard them. Rather, we want to analyze them in a spirit of *la vie philosophique*. Philosophy understands that we have deep metaphysical urges running through us. We also have the opposite. The philosopher Hegel can guide us here. As a dialectical thinker, he attempts to situate and clarify, we might say, both metaphysical and anti-metaphysical intuitions into a totality of a human life. Thus we can utilize Hegel with Freud to more deeply contemplate these intuitions. If we simply view existential intuitions as authoritative, they will turn into powerful id tools seducing us toward false standards of measurement. Without deep interpretation, without filtering existential intuitions through *notre nature profonde*, they threaten to become Siren songs. However when we let ourselves be directed by our highest human faculties, the same intuitions can help us evolve according to true standards. We can forge ourselves into splendid beings without sacrificing truth or abandoning our inner natures. Evolving means going through the layers of the self and the world to rebuild, from the rubble, lives of excellence. Hegel is close to perfect for getting things started.

Hegel argues that we begin our lives within and through a sort of oceanic oneness. Still this is only the beginning stage.[16] Existentially, it's a peaceful period with a child growing from a mother. There's no hard separation or conflict; it's perfectly natural. Hegel calls this first stage: undifferentiation and harmony. Humans come into the world literally attached to their mothers. This alone connects one to more than one's self. The umbilical cord and the mother's environment is a dwelling that keeps the child alive, even before it is sentient. This fact of literal attachment might initiate a primordial sense of connection that a self rediscovers, and perhaps misinterprets, after evolving into a feeling and contemplating self. What Freud's friend takes as a subjective "fact" is not really a fact. It's an interpretation of a feeling. It is not an unquestionable foundation. No metaphysical claim can simply be granted ontological privilege. For the self existed prior to any claim to metaphysical certainty, and we must ask ourselves about the origin and meaning of the intuitions we are interpreting, rather than simply assuming a supernatural or any other origin. Of course, a zygote, embryo, fetus, and then an infant will experience vicissitudes at each stage culminating in the cold shock of coming out of the cave. It's a coming out without Socratic self-knowing, but with a deep Heideggerian brick ready-to-hand, as one's comportment is already taking on a certain directionality. We are beings in space and time, such that even a pre-sentient being is developing a certain habitude and perspective that will continue to work, largely pre-reflectively, through the individual later in life.

The preborn child is part of the mother and is floating in what we might call an oceanic space. Still, this oneness is a lie. It's not a oneness. It can die without the mother dying, and vice versa. What it needs, and partly is, comes from the outside. A growing being mediates everything from the outside through an emerging self. What the mother eats, if she's stressed or not, her sleep, etc., shape the infant, yet each being will react somewhat uniquely. What's not unique is that we are all at the mercy of many forces. We are so vulnerable it's no wonder we later try to mask it. If things are unstable, perhaps the feeling of metaphysical oneness never arises or is weak. If the environment has relatively no conflict then perhaps a belief in wholeness continues to grow. Of course, it has to be more complicated than all this, but conceptually, albeit roughly, we can trace why certain ideas, beliefs, urges, feelings, and even needs arise in us. Further, we see how tricky it is to

---

[16] See Georg Wilhelm Friedrich Hegel, *Phenomenology of Spirit* (Oxford, 1977).

interpret it all. For not only is the "subjective fact" Freud's friend talks about not foundational, but nothing is. We never get back to some starting point. Every person was created and came from other created persons, and humans came from other organisms, which came from others, and so on. Whenever we might think we hit a foundation, it's always possible to go further back. Why the fetish with origins and foundations anyway? We all have agency. Not every great person had an unproblematic start in life. Often it's the opposite. These quests for anterior meanings are symptomatic.

Hegel and Freud understood that by the time we can contemplate metaphysics, we are out of the early infant stage of undifferentiation and harmony. By this point, we know that we are separate from our mother and we know that others, and the world itself, are not one with us. Hegel calls this second stage one of differentiation and disharmony. In other words, we now experience our lives as individuals, but there is conflict with others and the external world. Freud says this just is the human condition. What it means to be human is to be an individual trying to survive and to become somebody in the world you find yourself in. His work is about trying to help us manage it all. Hegel dreams of us evolving to a third stage of keeping our individuality but getting harmony back. Both Hegel and Freud would not be surprised that many have a metaphysical urge in them. Both theorists trace oneness back in time, with Hegel adding that it also comes from an urge for a greater future. Freud suggests it simply exposes one's unresolved past and lack of accepting the human condition.

Freud points out that even after we come to understand that the world and others are separate from us, we make the false step of thinking that we, ourselves, are simple and whole. We develop a sort of natural dualism between ourselves and the rest of the world. Still, as we regularly confuse the details between ourselves and the world, we are forced to acknowledge that life is even more complicated and uncertain. This makes us uncomfortable. It's unsettling to know that sometimes we confuse what comes from us with what comes from the outside. Sometimes what is really inside us we think is outside us. For instance, when my mood impacts how I view things. Perhaps, I only later realized it was me projecting my mood into the situation. Conversely, sometimes what's really outside us we think is in us, such as a desire that I think stems from my own being, might actually be what my mother or someone else desired for me. Again, later, I might realize it wasn't really something I cared about, but something I was expected to care about. Freud understands that these sorts of realizations don't magically happen. We have to work on ourselves to understand it all. Even after we understand, that's not the end of it.

For instance, even things we know are coming from inside us are not necessarily things we completely want. We understand that sometimes we have contradictory drives within us. There are layers to the self. We have a past and a history within us. We have varying powers and instincts fighting for control. One of the most powerful is an id force that seeks pleasure and doesn't seem to care about what's realistic. We also have an ego or rational part that is slow to develop but learns to push back on the id. There are cultural and social pressures too. Further, none of the past impulses, desires, or experiences just evaporate without a trace. We don't just mature once and for all. We don't just stop having irrational or unrealistic ideas, feelings, wishes, or needs. We don't completely change or get over things, even when we think we did. Finally, both the metaphysical urge and the anti-metaphysical urge live in us. Neither has plans of moving out any time soon. *Dans nos maisons*, the rent is cheap and one never knows who or what will be dropping in or popping up.

Freud uses the analogy of the Eternal City of Rome to explain the layers of the self. The self resembles a city that has an ancient past and has gone through generations of change, including war and peace, and everything in between. We can excavate some of it and some we cannot. Nonetheless any of it could potentially impact us under certain conditions. There are too many unknowns, but what we do know, Freud says, is that in our past we were helpless and completely dependent. As helpless and dependent, we reached out to whom and what could help us. Perhaps the father would save us. Then we realized the fiction of that. Fathers too are mortal and limited. Next we concocted the idea of Fate. If things are written in stone, then I might think that I can just relax and go with the flow. But this is too abstract and is contradicted by our sense of freedom. Thus, we invented various religions to help us make sense of the many fears, needs, and desires within us. The bottom line, for Freud, is that the oceanic feeling is just residual of our prior infantile cluelessness and helplessness. Due to this we can understand the urge to grant a "peculiar feeling"[17] immediate authority. A desire to believe that the feeling is adequate evidence to prove religion true is unsurprising. Yet to grant a desire or a feeling such authority is not defensible. It's natural to appeal to unqualified authorities, *non*? Still, *notre nature profonde* runs deeper. We must go deeper.

Freud shows us that even seemingly direct or simple intuitions, like the oceanic feeling, are already mediated interpretations emanating from us as historical beings living in an Eternal City. Viewed as authoritative, they are powerful id tools to seduce us toward false standards of valuation. They

---

[17] *Civilization and its Discontents*, p. 24.

promise a type of "power, success, and wealth" for those willing to sacrifice true happiness and deep meaning. Rather than looking at our lives through abstractions, and instead of searching for magical essences within us, what if we simply look at our real lives in their contexts? What if we try to live *la vie philosophique*? What if we choose noble activities and pursue excellence in accordance with them? If we are playing pickup basketball, and I start selecting players based on whether they claim to feel the oceanic feeling or not, I am operating by a false standard. The only relevant and coherent way of picking players, if I actually care about basketball excellence, is to choose the ones with the best basketball skills to fill my team. To be driven by any other considerations is absurd and renders basketball mediocre.

CHAPTER 2 — THE QUEST FOR HAPPINESS

> The common man cannot imagine this Providence otherwise than in the figure of an enormously exalted father. Only such a being can understand the needs of the children of men and be softened by their prayers and placated by the signs of their remorse. The whole thing is so patently infantile, so foreign to reality, that to anyone with a friendly attitude to humanity it is painful to think that the great majority of mortals will never be able to rise above this view of life.[18] —Sigmund Freud

Freud understands that we need to make sense of the world. Still, he has trouble accepting that most people will find this through the supernatural or in a religion. Traditional religions provide relatively simple answers to the riddles of life, give peace by allowing us to believe that someone is looking out for us, and allow us to hope that we can survive our death and end up in a better place. This is the image of God as the Father. Freud says this is infantile and acknowledges that since so many people accept some version of this belief, it creates a feeling of alienation toward humankind for anyone who isn't religious. The other problem for Freud, and perhaps a deeper one, is the fact that many who know that the standard religious stories are implausible will defend intellectualized variations of them. This is more depressing from Freud's standpoint. Of course, he understands that in the past one paid too big a price not to pretend to believe, but he finds it intellectually disingenuous, and a weakness, for modern educated people to perpetuate this falsehood. We can use Freud's own understanding of the mind, though, and say, even if we develop certain capacities, we may not develop others. Someone who has excellent reasoning skills in one area still may not be able to apply

---

[18] *Civilization and its Discontents*, p. 39.

strict rationality in other spheres so easily, especially concerning existential and ontological things.

Further, not everyone is courageous. We all have unresolved issues, so it shouldn't be too surprising that there is not exactly consistency across or throughout our lives. Plus, we don't want to underestimate today's social pressures. Social norms and social identities are, for most people, essentialist and metaphysically interpreted whether they realize it or not. That's part of the reason why today one still pays a big price if they explicitly turn against society's dominant norms and lifestyles. Of course, one doesn't end up in some medieval torture chamber, but we see how viciously some are attacked. Some people even lose their jobs and risk physical danger. Even those on the inside, the Pope for example, can only bend things so far. Hence, Freud warns the philosopher to be careful, for the true believers in God as Father will have little patience for sophisticated or intellectualized distortions of their beliefs. As he playfully warns, "Thou shalt not take the name of the Lord thy God in vain."[19] In other words, be careful in pretending or in performing in life. This is good advice, but it seems not to be heeded today, as performance is fashionable. Performing implies the need for an audience and suggests an interest in celebrity. Still, it has some philosophical justification.

The Performative

The idea that performance or the performative is essential to make sense of one's life might seem to follow from the death of the Cartesian subject. If there is no deeper self lurking behind the acting self, then there may be no grounding to appeal to outside of the visible self. As seen, performance itself becomes the house of meaning and takes center stage. This puts the emphasis on acting in new and different ways. *Différance* and playfulness, as externalized, become the signs of authenticity, and in themselves signal virtue, progress, and enlightenment. Although fashionable, one should be cautious with the performance metaphor. Life is a serious matter. Performance implies a show, entertainment, and fun.[20] But human life is not a show. And, for most people who have ever existed on this planet, life has not been entertaining or fun. Life has been and continues to be, for most, difficult. The metaphor is rather naive on many levels. On the philosophical level, the unsophistication takes the form of thinking that without a Cartesian subject at hand, perfor-

---

[19] Ibid., p. 40.

[20] The irony is that to inject seriousness into mere performances, performers must take themselves ultra-seriously. This distracts from the relevant questions of whether the activity is serious or whether that particular manner of performing is relevant to the context.

mance itself is automatically meaningful. But action itself is not inherently meaningful, and it's not just because meaning is *différé* as Derrida might say; rather it's because meaning is situational. A meaningful action is not something ready-made to be popped into a microwave and heated into coherent existence. Artificial food and artificial people exist whether or not there are fresh fruits or Cartesian selves on the menu. We need to look at the action in relation to the environment. Any action occurs in an already established place. Fabrication doesn't manufacture human meaning or coherent knowledge. We need to look beyond the performer to determine meaning. Of course, as an analytic exercise we can isolate anything. But if you chop off someone's hand it doesn't work anymore. The hand loses its human qualities. Still, you can perform an examination on a living hand without studying the rest of the body. Even so, in reality, the living hand only exists as part of a body and its usefulness and meaning cannot be understood except as part of something larger. To understand the meaning of that particular hand and that specific body, the living history and materiality of the individual matter. When we forget that knowledge only comes out of meaningful contexts, we risk reducing the concrete usefulness of something to abstract exchange-value.

I can sell a disembodied hand, but I cannot be useful or pursue excellence unless I can use my hands in appropriate ways. Making ourselves into performers we risk becoming interchangeable commodities. The self is objectified. Or as the French word *chosifier* (*chose* = thing) better captures it, the performative self is thing-like. An "object" has a sort of adornment to it. Whereas "thing" more readily signals an "inanimate object," and implies lifelessness. Pretending turns one into a thing; a culture of commodification socializes us with the language of stuff or things. The self becomes a thing. The performance is thing-like. This is all very playful. Still, a subject is not a thing. True life is not about acting or pretending; it's about developing our individual qualities and actualizing capabilities in relationship with others. This is done best through rich contexts grounded in rational histories. When we first start to engage with meaningful human traditions, it takes time to adapt to the new context. One cannot become something worthwhile overnight except in a shallow society operating via standards of untruth and manipulation. The Freudian quest is about *evolving* rather than transformation. *La vie philosophique* requires time and patience, it necessitates work and self reflection to evolve. Evolving is hard; much of it cannot be seen simply from the outside. Contemporary society operates against this philosophy of living. It functions according to the logic of immediate exterior transformation. Popping a pill, having a cosmetic surgery, buying new shoes, are as quick and easy as downloading an app. We create apps for everything. The app represents the miracle that religious people pray for. Whether it's a few words that makes one born again or a quick download, one is able to play at being transformed rather than working at growing. The app does the job. It's perfect for a society that cleanses itself through instant gratification. Our world is sophomoric, stuck in the traditional sophomore year, intellectually pretentious, overconfident, conceited, etc., but inside immature, lost, and awkward, as puberty is just kicking in.

When we consider the game of basketball we see evolution in progress. It's impossible to see coherent basketball by just throwing a ball to third graders and saying "play the game." Even with a year or two of practice they really don't understand basketball yet. Of course, these children might be more entertaining for us if they are members of our tribe or if we have an infantile understanding of this sport, but as basketball goes, it is not and cannot be excellent. Pretending to play basketball exposes the actors when they get on a court with real players. A caricature of a player is not a ball player. It's obvious for anyone who knows the game. Further, for those who take the game seriously it's disrespectful to dress up in shorts and a t-shirt and pretend to play around the court. However, in a society that rewards those who yell "it's me time," we miss the truth. Roaring is suited to a video clip society. Likewise, celebration of the new and of *différance en soi* doesn't require understanding, as this spectacle runs by the logic of commodities. This may produce id pleasure but it won't be a meaningful human activity.

Freud warned us about the temptation to pretend. But that's not to say that not pretending is always good or true either. Freud, following Nietzsche, harshly argues that anyone who dogmatically and sincerely asserts positive claims concerning God is weak and deluded. No one could have knowledge of the qualities and capabilities of God. At best, one can express hope of something beyond what we can see. It's a negative theological standpoint that is defensible. Jumping to positive attributes of such a foreign entity is a symptom of fear or trickery. At the same time, if spiritual belief does make you act better, and if you cannot be better without the belief, then you should keep taking the religious pills. Freud and Nietzsche hold that most people will need religion, of one sort or another. It's a decent medicine. Religion can redeem a life when someone tragically falls, and it is a route to a semblance of a meaningful existence. Freud insists, though, that individuals who choose one of the great monotheistic religions must be brave enough to say that they choose God because they need a God, and not waste intellectual or philo-sophical energy trying to rationalize it, otherwise they are just acting out.

Freud thinks that science and art can replace religion. He approvingly quotes Goethe's line that one "who possesses science and art also has religion; but he who possesses neither of those two, let him have religion!"[21] While Goethe's line is clever, it's not completely accurate. Science and art are useful in certain spheres but they are not replacements or the same as religion. We can say the same about them in relation to philosophy. Philosophy is guided by reason and free conversations between individuals. Both religion and philosophy ask questions about what one ought to do and who one should become. The answers cannot be found through scientific inquiry or simply within the imagination art invokes. Philosophy and religion search for meaning and coherence in terms of the whole of life, as well as constructing spaces for discovery of specific meanings and values of an autonomous individual. Ultimately, religion is the search to connect with a supernatural being or otherworldly space. Science rejects this quest, and tries to describe the natural world using specific tools and language, developed over time, with the goal of understanding how things operate and hoping to be able to predict and control aspects of the world. The arts expand the imagination and prioritize the aesthetic and beauty. Art does not need to limit itself to given reality in the way science must be grounded. Both science and art help us understand ourselves, but neither is independent of larger societal forces.

We sometimes forget that science is part of society. It seems to sidestep our cultural understanding of things, as it explains how the world as a whole operates according to the same physical, biological, and chemical processes. Supernatural beliefs and cultural ones don't seem to impact the temperature at which water boils. Furthermore, humans are part of the natural world and science positions us as part of it. Freud himself was a scientist and had confidence in it. Still, we can ask if science and technology are appropriate authorities when it comes to living by true standards. Can science and technology uncover the meaning of life? Can they create or discover happiness? Does actual existing technology help us avoid the false values of power, success, and wealth? Technology today seems to push us to use the world simply as a resource. Perhaps it distracts us from seeing our lives as meaningful. Further, when we understand nature and scientific laws, do we then understand what's moral and what's not moral, what's noble and what's base? Nature is not ethical, and science must ignore much of what we consider ethical to do its work. Science and technology are silent when it comes to pursuing what is noble and truly meaningful. When science forgets its mission or ignores its limitations, it lets itself become a slave to technology, it encourages nonthought, reification ("trust science"), and passivity in the public. As such, it

---

[21] *Civilization and its Discontents*, p. 40.

risks losing its nobility. When we hear statements such as "evidence-based research," we wonder if it really means that a corporation or social interest is driving the research toward a predetermined conclusion. Like priests embedded in the church during the Middle Ages, the scientist today is a little too comfortable in our identity-capitalist society.[22]

Art knows it is part of the social and political world. It prides itself on being a social construction. Being a social construction, one might argue that art is a unique power. The reasoning here is: if something is a social construction, that means humans made it, control it, and know it. If we made it, and it's unjust, we can change it or unmake it. This reasoning is fallacious. Just because we made something, it doesn't follow that we can control it or that we even know it. Anything we create is, in various ways, independent of us. If I make a chair, an *objet trouvé* along the lines of Duchamp, it now exists as an independent object. If I leave the room, the chair doesn't disappear. The chair can injure me if I trip over it. Maybe I can destroy the chair, or maybe a mountain lion will attack and kill me first, while I'm resting on the chair contemplating oceanic oneness. Even our social constructions, our artistic artifacts, exceed our absolute authority. Some things we make, we cannot unmake. Some things we did not make, we can, nonetheless, control. Anything we create can be used inappropriately. Parents create children, still they could use their children in inappropriate ways. The fact that something is a social construction only tells us that humans played a role in producing it. It doesn't make the thing less real or *a priori* tell us what it means. Art gives us no special ontological powers. Nonetheless we may allow it to have power over our imagination. We may forget art's nature and start to believe that fiction is true. Contemporary art and culture are suspect, as they are driven by money and politics, and have become mere entertainment. Mass art today is an industry. Its *raison d'être* is not to edify our souls or create beings in touch with their deep cultural roots. Rather, it's just candy for the id. It's a type of pretending that only scratches the surface of what art and culture could be and have been. Art is ideological. This is the danger of all performance-driven ideologies: they remain at the level of the surface, a mere artifact. Much of mass culture is sexuality pretending to be sensuality. We forget that sex is not one of our senses. Our society is confused. Art and mass culture are the vanguards of this. Our senses today, thanks to the culture industry, are reduced to one "sense" and it's not our most sensible one.

Freud was a materialist and he understood that ideas come from material reality. Ideologies gain control over us when we let them float too

---

[22] See Zeynep Pamuk, *Politics and Expertise: How to Use Science in a Democratic Society* (Princeton, 2021).

freely outside of material reality. Ideas are vital for us, though, and we have language to aid us in thinking through our ideas. Our ideas germinate through our language. Freud was one of the initiators of the "talking cure," as he understood the power of language. By talking, we can use language to know ourselves and to critique our ideas. Yet we often lose sight of reality and our lives when language itself becomes a force over us. It's ironic, as we need language to become fully human, but language can also reduce us to losing our sense of human reality. Fortunately, despite some contemporary roaring, language is not an insurmountable power necessarily controlling us. Language doesn't create material reality. There is a distinction between referring to something and the referent to which it is referring. An idea only has power, beyond being an idea, when people act on it. The power of language is subject to us. We have, when we try, lots of power over our words, and we can separate what we are experiencing from any particular word. We can even block out language in some situations. Language isn't as omnipresent to us as the environment. I can switch environments but I can never be completely outside of an environment. Still, no one seriously claims that space is a "prison-house." We can move in and out of environments, we can move in and out of different linguistic schemas and even, from time to time, completely sidestep language. Language does not dictate everything or even uniquely control us. An academic would have to be way up north to grant language that much power. Our beliefs can cause us trouble. Still, ideas and language arise from a deeper material reality, and they are shaped by our collective laboring history. Both as individuals and as collectives, we reshape our language and our relationship to it in complex ways. *Comme pour toutes choses*, some of this we control and some we cannot. Language is a power; so is a chair. Language can mediate our relationship to reality, but so can everything else. Language is not that special. It has no superpower. The Warrior fans yelling at Kyrie Irving in the 2016 NBA Championship game couldn't make him miss. Language didn't put a shield over the basket.

Still, it's probably impossible to imagine our human lives without language. Fortunately, we have language and so we ask: Why did science, art, religion, and philosophy develop in civilization? To help us understand our mortality? Do they play an important role in our survival, our needs, as well as our wants? Are they part of the quest to avoid pain, have pleasure, and perhaps even find happiness? Freud knows that life is tough and people will need to find ways to deal with existence. Life can be wonderful, but we all also find out, at some point, that it has "too many pains, disappointments and impossible tasks."[23] Life will kick you in the shorts one day, and

---

[23] *Civilization and its Discontents*, p. 41.

not necessarily when you see it coming. Freud wants to get to the root of our intellectual pursuits that only developed because, he thinks, we are creatures driven by trying to avoid pain and gain pleasure. He sidesteps any more high talk of the meaning of religion, philosophy, science, and art, and tries to situate them in basic drives of our organism. On this interpretation, pleasure and pain are the sources which give birth to "higher mental activities."[24] He formulates the ways we deal with these root sources by cataloging our response to pleasure and pain into three groups: "powerful deflections, which cause us to make light of our misery; substitutive satisfactions, which diminish it; and intoxicating substances, which make us insensitive to it."[25]

The Three Paths

1. Deflection

Freud argues that the most rational route to deal with the pain of existence is the route of deflection. By throwing ourselves into concrete and meaningful work we are giving ourselves, as directly as possible in civilization, the best chance to live a life that's less painful and it offers many pleasurable opportunities. Freud stresses that scientific labor is most aligned with the reality principle. Perhaps this is a personal projection in the way that Plato determined that philosophers are the most suited to be rulers. Still, the quest to understand nature and the way things work, both in our environment and within ourselves, is intrinsically interesting and instrumentally helpful. Science can ease suffering and can give us hope of further control and longevity. A related, but more practically focused, form of deflection comes out of the ending of Voltaire's *Candide*. "*Il faut cultiver notre jardin*,"[26] claims Candide at the end of his adventures. He learns not to expect much or ask for much and to simply cultivate his garden. A simple life, a slow life, that is concrete, focuses on hard work and values rooted relationships (even if they seem imperfect) is a recipe for more than a modicum of happiness. Working the soil in the name of growing food is noble. And doing so with those you have a history with and care about helps. You don't have to be exactly alike, though. Similar to Candide, we might be friends with someone who has to unrealistically philosophize or bring God into everything, and that's fine. Pangloss, the philosopher, claims that "we live in the

---

[24] Ibid., p. 69.
[25] Ibid., p. 41.
[26] Voltaire, *Candide* (Bordas, 1984) p. 184.

best of possible worlds."[27] To this, Candide responds, "All that is very well… but let us cultivate our garden."[28] The emphasis here is on the pronoun "us," as in "together." Even though their adventures have ended, they are still a community, a collectivity. It's a version of living that has proved useful, as it combines elements of both a Stoic life and an Epicurean one in the original senses.

The principles of Stoicism follow a sense of duty, while at the same time they teach us not to let things we can't control throw us off course. Marcus Aurelius reminded himself every morning that he would run into people who would try to cause him suffering. And he knew they would do so because they don't understand the true standards of life; they don't see what it means to live a good life. He made himself ready for it by cultivating his inner garden in which he built his citadel.[29] Both remained intact and unaffected. Conversely, Epicureanism shows us how to apply its principles in a rational way. The Epicureans found the beauty and simplicity of a garden as a worthwhile place to dwell in. They valued friendship and stressed the avoidance of pain, above the pursuit of intense and unnecessary pleasures. They were not hedonists. They ate simply and sensibly while not allowing themselves to get taken in by political and passionate stimulants. This allows for control of the self and forces the id to slow down and work with the individual. Studying and trying to incorporate elements of both Stoicism and Epicureanism can be part of a philosophical life. Both of these sets of principles tap into *la vie philosophique*. As living philosophies, they have deep yet differing views on metaphysics and God. As they sometimes have differing perspectives on how to live, knowing which to apply and when is a lesson in self-knowledge. When trying to be happy, evolve into someone higher, and find meaning, ancient philosophy offers a deep well.

Our tradition is on the path of human excellence, and Freud walks us further along. His emphasis is on work. We all know work is good for us. We

[27] Voltaire, *Candide*. Project Gutenberg, April 12, 2023, https://www.gutenberg.org/files/19942/19942-h/19942-h.htm#Page_161.

[28] Ibid.

[29] Marcus Aurelius, *Meditations*. Project Gutenberg, April 12, 2023, https://www.gutenberg.org/files/55317/55317-h/55317-h.htm. "When you wake up in the morning, tell yourself: the people I deal with today will be meddling, ungrateful, arrogant, dishonest, jealous and surly. They are like this because they can't tell good from evil. But I have seen the beauty of good, and the ugliness of evil, and have recognized that the wrongdoer has a nature related to my own — not of the same blood and birth, but the same mind, and possessing a share of the divine. And so none of them can hurt me. No one can implicate me in ugliness. Nor can I feel angry at my relative, or hate him. We were born to work together like feet, hands and eyes, like the two rows of teeth, upper and lower. To obstruct each other is unnatural. To feel anger at someone, to turn your back on him: these are unnatural."

need to work. Idleness will kill the evolving self. Beyond that, having friendships, love, and responsibilities to others and to ourselves can create meaningful environments and help one become mature and deep. Such deflections cultivate hope, while leaving room for irony, and Voltaire's manner of making light of our misery is a partial cure that helps to sustain one through a human life.

Freud himself doubts that the average person will find work as deflection sufficient. He claims that to really be successful, work must feel vitally important and allow one to be creative,and gain power. Only then will it diminish the pain of existence. Most jobs lack these features. Most people would quit their job if they were able to. In other words, work is not a deep source of meaning for most, and Freud thinks it's because most people are not self-driven or talented enough. This may be a little extreme, but is probably closer to the truth than the current mantra of "you can do anything" that's sold in the educational marketplace. Thus, before we dismiss Freud for being elitist we need to remember that he's talking about whether work and science are powerful enough deflections to push back on nihilism. Expecting a job to not only provide economic stability but also to be a cure for existential angst is asking a lot from it. This is why Freud doubts it will have universal success. Put otherwise, Freud seems to think that only certain jobs and certain people, truly, can find peace with the human condition through work. It's a view that even Plato probably wouldn't completely agree with, as Plato more heavily emphasizes one's role in the society. Today, we surely see the wisdom in stressing that if people find projects that suit their talents, and they recognize they are contributing to making the whole function rationally, then existential meaning might, at least, be approached.

2. Substitutive Satisfactions

According to Freud, "substitutive satisfactions," which diminish our misery, are fictions or illusions that provide contrast to a dull reality. Freud warns us of the power of artistic illusions (and we should add it's as much technological as artistic today). Although it's not real when stacked next to the deflective mode, it is nonetheless mentally effective thanks to the role of fantasy in our lives. Some call it escapism *à la Bovary*. Our inner life sometimes seems more real, and often more interesting, than the day-to-day grind. Substitutive satisfactions then diminish the pain of a sorry existence but may also diminish existence into something sorry. Thus, Freud can't advocate for it much. At his time it was easier to avoid too much socially-driven fantasy, as most people literally had to labor, and during labor they did not have access to radios, televisions, cell phones, etc. Thus, there was a type of natural differentiation between work and leisure. Today, these are more blended throughout our day. We might listen to the radio while driving to work, and there could be a television in the office waiting room or at the gym. Grabbing a drink after work with our friends, we might catch the game and, of course, everyone constantly checks their phones. Much of all this exposes us to manipulating fantasy. In other words, the realm of fantasy and illusion is now intertwined through the lifeworld; we don't just engage in escapism when in Vegas. But we don't want to overestimate this either. Technology or not, we are like Madame Bovary, in that we can access fantasy in our minds at will. Today and yesterday, individuals easily dive into the recesses of their minds. This starts in childhood and, probably, never goes away. It's one of the amazing aspects of being human. We even experience substantive satisfactions in our dreams; these experiences transcend our control. The lines between reality and fantasy are constantly being blurred and redrawn. In this way we see the ambiguity, the good and the bad, the hope and the waste, in aesthetic escapism.

If we look at this through Freudian categories we can say the id, as driven by the pleasure principle, is something we are continually in danger of rushing back to. But it's not quite accurate to say "in danger." For sometimes utilizing the id is what saves us. But in general, Freud is warning us: if we wish to avoid pain and have pleasure, the unfiltered id is problematic, as it has a problem with reality. To get consistent with reality we need the infantile instinct to be filtered through the ego and superego. With a successful sublimation, both ego and superego will put into our consciousness a path to satisfying the id desire in a socially acceptable way. For example, what starts as an unconscious biological need, say hunger, begins working in us before we are conscious of it. I have money in my pocket. There is a KFC across the street. The smell of fried chicken permeates the air. By the time the instinct reaches my consciousness I immediately think of grabbing some fast food as opposed to stealing my neighbor's lunch. In fact, stealing my neighbor's lunch is something I may not really have thought of. But for some reason it crossed my mind that particular day. From now on, when reality becomes dull, the thought of lifting someone's lunch can provide me with an occasional private chuckle. In any case, driving through KFC is a successful sublimation. I don't have to repress my hunger or let it out in a non-civilized way. However, is it really a successful sublimation? Did I really satisfy my biological need that prompted a feeling of hunger? It seems one should say "yes," as I'm not hungry anymore. But perhaps fast food is merely satisfying an id desire to eat something yummy but not satisfying the body's need for nutrients. My true need and deeper human desire is health and longevity. My feeling of hunger is signaling a need for healthy energy. Yet my childish instinct and society's norms tell me I'm being rational. I'm clearly being consistent with the way our world works; I'm not going to get arrested for what I'm eating. My action was practical and seemingly moral. But does the world work properly? Is our world broken? Isn't regularly eating fast food poisonous to the body and mind? Isn't the American diet unhealthy? Doesn't it increase one's chances of getting illnesses ranging from diabetes to Alzheimer's? Further, aren't its practices immoral if you care about sentient suffering? Aren't our American commercial food industry and factory farming as unethical as can be? What if pretty much every sphere in this country is now driven by the same logic and under the same schema? What if the norms that society socializes us to believe are rational and morally acceptable truly aren't? *Oh, là là!*

Certain foods are unhealthy, especially if consumed regularly. Our bodies don't thrive by just eating anything and in any amount. Drinking water intrinsically helps the body function properly. Drinking too much damages the kidneys; drinking too little dehydrates the body. Even innocuous activities must be rationally regulated. Further, certain activities are by nature wrong and bad for humans wanting to be humane. A club that tortures cats or children on the weekends shouldn't exist. Putting poison into one's mind or body intrinsically harms the mind and body. When food becomes, first and foremost, about making the id feel good, instead of nourishing our organs and muscles, then it is a substitutive satisfaction. There's nothing wrong with eating things that taste good, but eating is, above all else, supposed to be for keeping us alive. We shouldn't sacrifice health and strength just to satisfy id food cravings. Eating is a biological and historical activity. In a dignified society we would focus on producing food that makes us live longer and that develops our senses to give us deeper human pleasure. After eating to survive, we should be eating to experience the human condition in all its beauty, richness, and potential. For example, when learning how to read, we have to start simple. We should put good books into children's hands and minds with the hope that one day they can read books with the sophistication and beauty of Marcel Proust. At the same time if we read trashy works, if we insist on gobbling dumb shows, aren't we remaining in the infantile stage? Aren't we being controlled by our id? The food industry, and others, are outwitting us. The activities we engage in need to adhere to their proper justification, or they risk becoming not worthwhile. If a good activity starts to change the values by which it runs, it risks losing its goodness or it becomes another activity. If I am allowed to punch you in the face when you are shooting a three pointer in a basketball game, then basketball has become a UFC sport. If in academia, the ability to freely pursue truth and knowledge gives way to something else, then academia is dead. Eating a pseudo-food meal is not a successful sublimation. The food isn't serving the body just as today's universities are at risk of becoming pseudo-educational marketplaces incapable of serving up truth or the other academic and intellectual values. It's all performative. One can ask the question, is contemporary America's over-arching schema itself is a substitutive satisfaction? And if so, who are we really?

3. Intoxicating Substances

Freud's final matter of coping doesn't require many words, beyond reiterating the dangers. We all know the dangers of intoxicating substances, and we all know they are a direct way to make one insensitive to the pains we all experience. There are many intoxicating substances that are so powerful they are almost irresistible. We all have weaknesses, so one or the other substance can catch us. For one person it might be alcohol, another drugs. For someone else it could be gambling. There are just too many tempting substances in the modern world. Often we don't realize the power and control intoxicating substances have on us until it's too late. From shopping to tanning, to tattoos and body piercing, seemingly anything can become a serious addiction. Further, we have decided, it seems, to stop pretending that we can do without, what we might call, the vices. The modern world is embracing the subhuman. There's a certain honesty in this. Legalization of marijuana is the model here: it's everywhere and it's accessible, as is alcohol, to everyone. Again, this is somewhat honest, as marijuana seems no worse than alcohol. But it does tend to stink up the place. Like a perfume, weed is now the CHANEL No. 5. The odor is ubiquitous in Southern California. Besides the odor, one cannot help suspecting that this experiment is all going to end badly. Legalization is probably not a great long-term plan, as history has shown we don't tend to grow deeper and more sophisticated by giving in to id pleasures. It does not grow stronger individuals or teach the virtue of aiming to have a noble reputation. Making id pleasures socially acceptable and readily accessible is just an excuse to be infantile and a ploy for some to make money. This strategy may cause us to crumble.

Freud utilizes The Eternal City to good effect, in Chapter One of *Civilization and its Discontents*, for showing, analogically, how the layers of the self and a city survive in one form or another. But here we should just point out the obvious fall of Ancient Rome. Will our time come? Have we already accepted it? Are there just too many temptations? There's an ancient story about a king who asked for something that would make him happy when he was sad, and sad when he was happy. Someone gave him a ring inscribed with

"This too shall pass." Our future is not determined. Many individuals and some groups continue to try to create environments and lives that reject the cult of intoxicating substances. This is where one needs to stand up as an individual. For those with power, success, and wealth are the ones pushing intoxicating substances the hardest. They are the ones telling us to lighten up and to light up. Selling false standards of living is cool as evidenced by the artists, actors, and athletes willing to promote drinking and other intoxicating substances through commercials and such. They sell their human selves for a few bucks in the service of their corporate masters. Intoxicating substances are still winning.

Still, it's worth having the television on if there's a good game on TNT. Basketball can be a tool to help one deal with life, and it can satisfy, pretty much as well as anything today can, any of the three categories that Freud walks us through. Basketball today can be a rational deflection. There are lots of well-paying jobs at all levels of the sport and the spheres connected to it. People today are socialized, or reduced, depending how you look at it, to find all this meaningful and stimulating. As a practice itself, basketball is an activity that one can spend much time on, both alone and with others, trying to master. Practicing the skills of shooting, passing, jumping, playing defense and so on are healthy for the body. Further, in our society, if you become pretty good, you get recognition from others. The highlight for many in our society is the time spent during high school sports. Shooting hoops can be done most of one's lifetime. There are leagues with athletes in their 60's and older still playing decent ball. Many of us have sedentary jobs, so getting on the court in the evenings or weekends is refreshing. It connects the generations as we pass the sport on, not just to our sons but also to our daughters. It teaches the skills of competition and cooperation, of individuality and collectivity. Much of the globe has discovered the beauty of the game, and this sort of internationalism is a good thing.

Just as basketball can become a rational deflection when you look at the lives of Phil Jackson, Greg Popovich, and Steve Kerr, watching basketball and having a team to root for can be a substantive satisfaction. It has the potential to be a healthy, relaxing activity and can connect us with others who watch it, even though in reality the outcomes of the games have no bearing on our actual lives. For instance, Lakers fans and Clipper fans are serious about their teams. It's almost a religion as some cry over losses and celebrate victories as though they were the ones on the court. Situated properly in a human life, it can be a decent way to recharge. It's got positive cultural and artistic elements that bring beauty into the world. It can even be a social identity. People identify with their team and talk about it almost as if they believe it's an essential identity.

Of course, a Clipper fan could never imagine becoming a Lakers fan, and vice versa. Regardless there is no deep, true, or essential Clipper self inside of anyone. If I go to a funeral and someone asks me who I am, it is absurd to say "I'm a Clippers fan." No, in the context of a funeral, the meaning of the question is related to my relationship to whoever died.[30] Unless my relationship to the deceased was through the Clippers organization, it's meaningless to bring in the Clippers. If I turn this identity into something more, or if society does, then something has gone terribly wrong. When it comes to essentializing, we need to pull back rather than double down. Unless we are into totalitarianism.

It's easy to let identities become totalizing. It's also easy to turn them into brands in our capitalist society. Rather than working on ourselves, we brand and rebrand. Pornography is in the process of being rebranded. Should it be considered art? After all, it's just performance, *non*? It's just fiction, right? Should we think of porn as merely a hobby? It reduces sex to a hobby. It also kills one's ability to love, destroys those acting in it, and corrupts those consuming it. Porn is a poisonous, addictive substance which treats people, especially women, as products. It's astonishing that today many on the left attempt to defend this perversion.[31] Perhaps liberal consent, diversity, and freedom ideology is the theory of which OnlyFans is the practice. When one cannot distinguish a liberal feminist from the Marquis de Sade, one can only conclude that the capitalist schema is complete.

Freud warns us that sexual de-sublimation is a false and dangerous answer to the problem of the id. Sublimation is a better route. Turning towards higher activities of seeking knowledge and wisdom, connecting with family and friends, and putting beauty into yourself and the world won't get as many likes but you may end up liking yourself. For when we interact with the highest works of human achievement, we also connect with the true principles of things. They show us how life can go off the rails and point us in the human direction. We feel this in Tolstoy's very first line of *Anna Karenina*: "Happy families are all alike; every unhappy family is unhappy in its own way." America, despite its self-advertising, presents itself as a resentful and unhappy land. It's a place that is quickly ensuring there is no place in it for true art such as Tolstoy's, and no place for true lives either.

---

[30] This example was inspired by Georgia Warnke's article "We Need a more Context Sensitive Understanding of Identity." In *Areo*, 07/12/2020. https://areomagazine.com/2020/12/07/we-need-a-more-context-sensitive-understanding-of-identity/
[31] See Louise Perry, *The Case Against The Sexual Revolution* (Polity, 2022).

Beyond the Pain

Freud's focus on religion, which opens his second chapter, stems from his view that, for thinking people, religion cannot solve the theoretical puzzles of human existence nor the practical issues of avoiding pain. Freud trusts most in science, but he sees how high art is necessary. What he doesn't talk about though, except to warn the theologically-inspired philosopher, is the role of philosophy in coming to terms with the human condition. In fact, he seems not to trust much in philosophical speculation. Nonetheless, he cannot escape thinking about the meaning of life. After exploring the three measures for dealing with human suffering, he returns to the fundamental question of the purpose of human life. He concludes that this has not been given a satisfactory answer and that it may not have one. He sidesteps much in the philosophical tradition while engaging in his own philosophical musings. He points out that many people think that if life has no purpose, it would lose all value for us. Freud doubts this, and reminds us that one doesn't have to situate animals in some grand schema of the universe in order to see that an animal's life is not meaningless. We can extend this, and say that, from one perspective, even a plant's or a mountain's existence is not meaningless. Still, we do seem to view our existence differently. We have an instinct to view our lives as central to the meaning of everything, and yet we also can't deny that the universe is much bigger than we are, and we know that many animals on the planet are not here simply for our benefit. There is a contradiction in our thinking. We are able to appreciate the larger world, and things not directly connected to our lives. We take them for what they are, and see the beauty and intrinsic worth of much of the world. We don't question their right to be, or assume their existence is problematic unless we can ascribe a transcendent meaning to them. At the same time we impose this higher standard on ourselves.

We think that if there isn't something greater going on behind the scenes, then human life is meaningless. Freud accepts this on one level himself. He surprisingly concurs with the view that only religion could answer the question of "what is the purpose of life."[32] He adds that since no religion has offered a plausible story of the purpose of life, in his view, then there is no answer to the purpose or meaning of life. It's an interesting argument. Children often give supremacy to their fathers: only my dad knows the answer to my questions. When approached, the adult may respond: I don't know. Or he may try to come up with answers, which are unsatisfactory. The child then realizes that if my dad doesn't know, if he cannot provide me adequate answers, then

---

[32] *Civilization and its Discontents*, p. 42.

no one knows, no one can help me. This is analogous to Freud's claim that if life had meaning, only religion would know what it is, and religion doesn't know what it is, so life has no meaning.

Freud reasons like a philosopher. However, Freud is not an authority on philosophy. Nietzsche, on the other hand, is. He may respond to Freud in the following manner: If "the meaning of life" were something to be discovered or not discovered, and *if only* religion could in principle discover it, then if religion can't find it, you might be right to conclude that there is no meaning to life. Nietzsche might add that Freud is assuming two problematic points. First, religion (and your dad) may not be the best authority on the meaning of life; there may be other people or disciplines better suited for the quest. Religion might be pretty good at pretending or parallel playing, as on a playground full of toddlers, but it is not serious. Second, the meaning of life might not be something one could "discover." Nietzsche rejects the premise that the meaning of life is something that one could find or not find, as in a scavenger hunt. It's a waste of time and effort. The meaning of life must be created. For Nietzsche, only a few talented individuals, and perhaps a few groups, can achieve this art form: creating lives of meaning. One does not find or discover the meaning of life, as in magic or a miracle. It's a project that requires authenticity, a genuine ambition.[33]

Since Freud doesn't share Nietzsche's view on the meaning of life, he poses a different question: Is life worth living? A religious person might link the two questions. They might say that life is worth living only because it's the meaning of life (determined by God) that affords individuals the chance to get to heaven and live an eternal happily ever after. What if you miss the mark? You may change your mind and decide, too late, that life wasn't worth living, because the meaning of life landed you in an eternal unhappiness. Unlike the religious person, Freud wants to pursue the question as to whether life is worth living without bringing God into the answer. He also dismisses the theoretical questions of the meaning and purpose of human life.[34]

Albert Camus too was fixated on the question of whether life is worth living from an atheist perspective. He concluded that the question of suicide was the fundamental philosophical question we must ask ourselves.[35] If one

---

[33] See Nietzsche, *Beyond Good and Evil* (Vintage, 1989), *Thus Spoke Zarathustra*, in *The Portable Nietzsche* (Penguin, 1982).

[34] Freud tends to equate "purpose in life" and "meaning of life." He claims we can only intelligible speak of our life having a purpose or there being a meaning to life if there were an agent that created us and gave us a purpose or meaning. We can follow Freud in using purpose and meaning in the same sense but, following Nietzsche, reject his conclusion that an outside agent is necessary for human life to have meaning or purpose.

[35] Albert Camus, *The Myth of Sisyphus* (Vintage, 1942).

concludes that life is worth living, then live it. If one concludes that life is not worth living, one has the right to end his or her life. Suicide is serious business, and if you are contemplating it, you need to communicate with others before doing anything rash. Suicide is the end of life in a way that other things don't end. I can lose my hat forever, but it's something essentially different to lose my life forever. If I lose my hat, it can be gone forever, but I can get another hat or live without a hat. However, when I die, I lose everything. In this way, the question of whether life is worth living or not is as central as Camus stated. You can lose direction in life but you can get direction back. When you lose your life, you don't get back your life. In fact, losing direction in life is expected and can be a positive thing, for a spell. In this way, it's less permanent or less of a loss than losing a hat. If I lose direction in life, it probably won't be gone forever in the same way that a hat can disappear. For so long as I am alive, I am always living in some direction, regardless of whether I feel I am lost or not. I may think my life has no direction, but it's never completely true. Nihilism is not really the absolute danger many think it is. For one is never completely nihilistic. We always believe in certain things, but maybe just not the things that others think necessary not to be nihilistic. Others might say, if I don't believe in God that makes me a nihilist, suggesting that *they* need God to make sense of their lives. Still, believing in God doesn't dictate whether it's worth taking care of your kids, or rooting for your team, or eating at In-n-Out. In other words, one may still believe that life is worth living even when going through an existential crisis. Oftentimes, God as the answer arises, after the crisis of nihilism. This can be perceived as a mechanism to handle the pain of existence. Freud is right, we can intelligibly ask the question of whether "is my life worth living" without worrying about the question "what is the meaning of life."

Claiming that there would be no morality without God also suggests that we are admitting that we need a God to be moral. If we cannot imagine a world of morality without God, or if we cannot imagine acting morally unless we think a God is watching, aren't we unwittingly admitting something about ourselves? We don't know if God exists or not. We do know that the world has morality and immorality in it. If we found out tomorrow, with absolute certainty, that God does exist, would everyone be moral tomorrow, and the next day? If we found out tomorrow, with absolute certainty, that God doesn't exist, would everyone become immoral? What if we found out the Manicheans were right, and there exist two equally powerful gods, one moral and one immoral? Pinning morality or nihilism on whether God exists or not is a type of wish fulfillment. One wants there to be a God and then appeals to arguments about morality or nihilism to satisfy the wish. These beliefs are within the Freudian category of "wish fulfillment," but they are not logical points or true claims about reality.

As we've seen, Freud gives up on the meaning of life question and turns to a less ambitious, and more empirical grounded one: what people show by their actual behavior is the purpose and intention of their lives. In regard to our behavior he asks: what do we see individuals expecting from life? What are they hoping to achieve in it? His answers follow the great tradition of Plato and Aristotle: we strive for happiness. This striving is two-fold: we exert ourselves to avoid pain or we maximize pleasure. Depending on our constitution, physically and mentally, we might prefer striving more to avoid pain or we might be more inclined to reach out to pleasure. In either case, the goal is happiness. Freud thinks that if we could, we would let ourselves be completely driven by the pleasure principle. Without the reality principle to check it, the id would maintain its dominance inside of us and we would not develop other attributes or human qualities. We only develop into creatures more complex than id machines because the external world forces us to. Reality is not conducive to an id life of pure pleasure. That would destroy us very quickly. Reality is a cold, hard place. We are forced to adjust to reality, and it is reality that thwarts our quest for a life of pure pleasure. At the same time Freud warns us that deep down we regret and resent that we had to give up the id quest. Still, reality isn't so horrible that we cannot turn to a quest for happiness. Happiness is a goal that allows us to hold on to a decent amount of id pleasure, and it is consistent with trying to avoid much of the pain of existence. Happiness is an extended or revised quest, formulated after the initial plan fails. Therefore, it might be thought of as a plan B. Plan A, unlimited, never-ending pleasure, was a fantasy; but plan B, moments of pleasure over the course of a life, has a chance for success. And when plan B seems hopeless, it's time to read Camus.

As we have seen, according to Freud the pleasure principle, due to the demands of the external world, gives ground to the more modest reality principle. Reality conditions us to accept some pain and to accept limited pleasure, and then gets us to interpret our existence as happy if this works out. So people might think themselves happy by merely having escaped extreme pain or by merely having a modicum of pleasure. Freud points out that this notion of happiness is partly based on biology, and partly on the state of reality at the time. For example, in some contexts, simply avoiding suffering can push the need or desire to obtain positive pleasure into the background. We all experienced this in trying to avoid catching COVID-19. Then, as the initial panic over COVID slowly turned into something we could start to live with, people were thrilled with just adding back the simple pleasures. Going to the places one took for granted before COVID took on a new significance and provided us with more pleasure than before. Others wanted to make up for the perceived or real loss of pleasure in confinement, and boomeranged the pleasure/pain instincts into an urge to live hard. COVID pushed many of us to think about what we want from life; and by shifting the environments we could inhabit, we got a firsthand taste of our life away from certain people and places and what it means concretely not to be able to do certain things or go to certain places.

Those who felt a strong urge to live fast and hard after lockdown were driven by the instinct that Freud calls an urge for an "unrestricted satisfaction of every need."[36] This is an attempt to get as close as possible to a version of plan A from above. Full-on pleasure emanating from the id. Freud would not be surprised that this presented itself as one of the most enticing methods of conducting one's life after a period of restraint. However, this strategy of putting enjoyment before caution, as many have found out, brings its own punishment with it. Whether it was catching COVID from going to the bar or purchasing a house that one later regrets, or jumping into a problematic relationship, or changing jobs or moving to another city, things didn't always turn out positively. Pushing hard for pleasure is a high risk quest.

Those who didn't pivot toward hedonism felt the power and calm that comes with avoiding displeasure and decided that lockdown was an acceptable way of life for them. That being the case, many still have adopted a philosophy of voluntary isolation after the pandemic. Freud understands how this gives one the happiness of quietness. When the external world loses its appeal, many, if able to, will turn away from the external world and reject it as necessary to make life worth living. And with Amazon delivering everything straight to the door, many have found this to be *pretty pretty pretty good* (read in your best Larry David voice). Plus, in a world that loves labels, it seems pretty cool to say "I'm a hermit" when someone asks you who you are.

Freud understands the intuition to avoid civilization, but he says it's smarter and healthier to become a member of a human community. A community can protect individuals and allow them to pursue robust projects that only are possible in external environments. In Freudian language, it is more consistent with the reality principle. Once one turns away from the trap of the pleasure principle, Freud encourages a full pivot to the reality principle. This is the reason he advocates for work that is socially validated, that stimulates and fatigues both mind and body. Filling your life working, having a family and friends, and engaging in little doses of leisure activities

---

[36] *Civilization and its Discontents*, p. 44.

that are innocuous (seemingly innocuous, like smoking an occasional cigar) is his preferred recipe for happiness.

Today, what do most people think about Freud's promise of happiness? A lot has changed since 1930. With today's technology, modern homes, virtual spaces, and societies changing norms we notice that people can create multifarious ways of occupying themselves. And there's not just the choice of staying in or going out. Today, we can stay in while we go out. People can connect to individuals and communities in places far away from the comfort of their homes. Of course, there are new risks. Sometimes these individuals and groups online are not who or what one thinks they are. Catfishing is common and seems to exist as a continuum in the virtual environment. In fact, even if one grew up in a small, connected, and friendly village, there is still the question of whether we actually know who and what those around us are. Besides, any group can turn on an individual. Even family. Certainly in our "cancel culture" we understand that no one is safe, and that the rules and norms of acceptability can shift overnight. And it's not just our time. History shows that many people are willing collaborators to almost any ideology or power under certain conditions. Hence, calculating the pros and cons of isolation versus joining a human community is complicated. Just the same we should mention that without human community the path of voluntary isolation doesn't really work. I need Amazon if I want to stay alone in my house. Similarly, buying a plot of land away from everyone and everything may work for a few people, but most of us don't have the skills anymore to survive off the land. Further, as in times past, a group of one hundred menacing men on horses (so to speak) could ride up to the gate. Life's a risk.

Although Freud gives us instructions to achieve the promise of happiness, he is pessimistic concerning its success. "The programme of becoming happy, which the pleasure principle imposes on us, cannot be fulfilled; yet we must not—indeed, we cannot—give up our efforts to bring it nearer to fulfillment by some means or other."[37] "Happiness, in the reduced sense in which we recognize it as possible, is a problem of the economics of the individual's libido."[38] It seems we have very little control. We can't completely transcend the wish of infantile pleasure, and reality-based pleasure is determined by a libido we didn't choose and can't really control. We understand now why Freud is skeptical of philosophy. Without a God, the only purpose for an organism like us is pleasure. Making sure one's pleasure doesn't violate the reality principle is the only theoretical guidance one needs. "There is no

---

[37] Ibid., p. 54.
[38] Ibid.

golden rule which applies to everyone: every man must find out for himself in what particular fashion he can be saved."[39]

Plato sees the human condition differently. He defines happiness as something qualitatively different than pain avoidance and pleasure achievement. He sees hedonism, even vanilla hedonism, as reckless. In the *Republic*, he refutes the hedonistic view that pleasure makes life worth living. As Plato points out in Book VI, pleasure in itself is not good, only pleasure linked to something higher or meaningful is good. Random pleasure doesn't make life worth living or give purpose. Not all pleasures are good, some are bad. Further, some pleasures lead to greater pains. To understand the value of pleasure, one needs a standard outside of pleasure and outside of hedonism itself. Pleasure has to link to something worthwhile to be meaningful and purposeful.

Trying to understand the effort and the meaning of a basketball team working hard to win a Championship in the NBA, we cannot capture its essence if we think only in terms of pleasure and pain. Trying to calculate how much pain the players go through, and trying to determine the pleasure in winning is to miss the whole point. The meaning is a collective, social meaning. It's not everyone determining things for themselves. Sports excellence is painful. The training of the body and mind hurts. If the goal was avoiding pain, then no one would be a great athlete. Additionally the happiness of achieving a Championship is a human happiness that gives one's life meaning and direction, and it is internally connected to others. Framing one's life in terms of higher goals and intersubjective projects is what gives human life its form and leads to happiness. Happiness is knowing yourself and what you have accomplished. It means thriving in various virtuous contexts, while pushing a thread of greatness through them all. It's a type of usefulness and excellence that's not reducible to an organism's pleasure and pain threshold. *La vie philosophique* understands this, but Freud as scientist sometimes falls into biologism and loses sight of the truth.

---

[39] Ibid.

CHAPTER 3 — THE CIVILIZATION TRAP

> This contention holds that what we call our civilization is largely responsible for our misery, and that we should be happier if we gave it up and returned to primitive conditions.[40]
> — Sigmund Freud

In the beginning of Chapter Three of *Civilization and its Discontents*, Freud reminds us of the difficulty of the quest for happiness. He highlights three sources of suffering: nature, our bodies, and people, in order to illustrate how they work together and separately, to cause our lives pain, which limit and restrict us. Given that suffering from nature and our bodies seem unavoidable, one might think it would be easier to accept the pain experienced from them. We all know the natural world can be hostile, and we know that our physical bodies injure easily, frequently become ill, and are subject to the natural processes of decay. It's not something we can really take personally. Nature and the elements impact us all, and everyone's body ages along a similar path. There's really no one to blame.

In fact, the limits we encounter from the greater power of nature or the feebleness of our own bodies "points the direction for our activity."[41] We plan our lives around the weather forecast and the seasons give us a sense of change and time on this planet. We avoid dangerous environments and hike in areas relatively safe, or we prepare for the vicissitudes we know await us. Furthermore, knowing how the body works, and what ultimately happens to it, helps frame our lives. When our bodies are young, we can run around and play. We do not think about the future. Then we realize it's time to grow up, to fall in love, to have children, to help the next generation, and so on.

---

[40] Sigmund Freud, *Civilization and its Discontents* (Norton Press, 2010), p. 58.
[41] Ibid., p. 57.

Our bodies and the way nature works condition much of what we are willing to risk. We look back at our youth and we look ahead to our future. If one lived a fortunate life, there is much to remember joyfully and much to hope for. If not, we contemplate our past as missed opportunities or mistakes. Some have regrets, some acknowledge they could have lived differently, and hopefully, try to help others avoid making the same errors. Overall, these limits and barriers need not be interpreted in a negative light. In fact, they are the conditions that make human life what it is; they are a central part of what it means to be human.

However, when it comes to intersubjective relationships we typically feel the suffering in a different way, for it tends to stick with us and grind in our minds. For instance, it's one thing to wake up feeling good and then have a rainstorm make you late for work. It's altogether another thing to start your day well and have it spoiled because someone treated you badly. It's a bummer when you cannot go to a party because you caught COVID. It's a whole different feeling when you have to stay home because you find out someone you thought was your friend has been messing around with your boyfriend or spreading vicious rumors about you. In social suffering one might think that willpower and attitude can mediate. We know the cold outer world and our vulnerable bodies will betray us, but we think and expect that we (ourselves and other people) should be able to act decently toward each other. As Freud puts it, we can't help thinking that the social rules and limits that humans themselves have imposed on ourselves should "be a protection and a benefit for every one of us."[42] Really, how hard is it to be nice to each other, to be nice to oneself? It turns out, quite hard. Plus, we quickly realize that things are not so simple. To live with and around others requires holding back on various instincts. It means delaying gratification and often, letting certain things go. As this continues, things get backed up inside of us. Some of it we always remember and some of it impacts us without our realizing it.

With all this occurring it's easy to shoot oneself in the foot and easier still to, so to speak, punch someone else in the gut. This sort of behavior is not limited to one group or certain individuals. We all hurt and harm: ourselves and others. We suffer on all social levels, from the family to the state and throughout society. Is it because we are ignorant, wicked, or more powerless than we think? This puzzle fascinates Freud. However, before answering this question we should spend some time on nature and our bodies as sources of suffering. Although Freud doesn't ponder upon them, we might think about these slightly differently in our time than he did in his.

---

[42] Ibid., p. 58.

Competing with the Sources of Suffering

Today, as science and technology have progressed, we have changed our relationship to them. We have new expectations when it comes to the external world and our bodies. Today, we believe we have more control and power than before, and, at the same time, arguably, we have become less in tune with both our environment and our bodies. Today, we are more willing to try to power through natural and bodily barriers to get what we want. We don't care if we live in the desert — if we want a lawn with green grass, we find a way to have it. We exploit technology to satisfy desires that could and should be either repressed or delayed. Repressing or delaying gratification has become, in America, a sign of weakness or a proof of failure. Our society's obsession with competition and winning has extended to include comparing which individuals and groups suffer the most. All decent humans suffer all the way down to their Being. To reduce human suffering to a contest is ridiculous and harmful, to everyone. Competition is everywhere: on television, on the playground, in schools, in universities, in families... America thrives on competition. But is it really such a good thing? Does this help our quest for happiness? Or is it symptomatic of something else?

Competition has progressed to the point where one need not develop human skills to prove oneself a winner. Tossing a bean bag, for instance, might get one on ESPN; being willing to go on television to turn your love and your life into a game show has gained tremendous popularity; blabbing about how hard or how perfect my life is has become part of the internet sport. This type of competition indicates an emptiness that we feel inside of us, a void that we must fill to feel alive. The fast fix is sold by the false values. Meaningless competition prevents us from understanding the meaning of life. Embracing false values and standards hinders us from living. When winning becomes everything and is gained at any cost, true happiness loses.

It is now even fashionable to say that merit is a sham. There's a competition to find reasons to deny individuals their accomplishments and to rationalize those who don't step up. We compete to label others as having some advantage that explains their success, and we do so, almost always, without really knowing anything about them. America loves brands and labels. We stick them on products and on people using cheap athletic wear glue. Instead of growing and evolving, we change the meaning of things to get what we want. It's all abstract and metaphysical banter, for America thinks only in terms of money and spirits, which reduces everything to this binary, ironically often led by those claiming to be critiquing dualism. We live in a surface society that throws around lazy concepts in order to judge each other according to the day's social artifices, by chicanery that colonizes the contemporary mind. In such a world, merit is not merited and all structures are suspect. By this definition, the NBA reeks of inequity. The average height of an NBA player is over six feet six inches. Those who succeed have unearned physical advantages, and most grow up in a privileged basketball culture that values and teaches the skills. Those who make it utilize generational knowledge and practice exclusion to maintain privilege. It's clearly structured to exclude most people, even most great athletes, in favor of a small minority of individuals. The players willingly, albeit playfully, admit this as they frequently make the "too small" gesture after scoring on an opponent. Maybe we should raise the rim to 20 feet or lower it to 5 feet. Perhaps, we can make the floor uneven or larger, or smaller. Should we change the size of the ball, or make it softer? We could attach weights to the high fliers and give flubber shoes to those who cannot jump. Whatever we do, some will gain an advantage and some will not. There will be structural bias. Is professional basketball bogus? Should we not respect the years of practice and deep sacrifice of those who made it into the NBA? Should we dismantle the whole thing?

It's impossible to deny the greatness of NBA players. Individuals who cannot be great, and resent it, will take over the realms where authentic greatness is not clearly visible. Thus they make themselves visible by roaring. What's roaring worth on a basketball court? You still missed the shot. Roaring is often a strategy to deny the complexity of the world and of our history. A society that constantly compares itself to others or looks for loopholes to deny others is not a good society. Those driving this attitude are missing their shot to live a decent human life. They are making the world worse and it's a sign of their emptiness. People without virtue don't care, though. All they want is their win. America will give them their win, if it suits the market. In this way, being labeled a "loser" in American society might mean that you are not. It might suggest that you don't define yourself by the brand of car you drive or any other abstract social identity. It might signify that you are an individual who is living in accordance with the higher world and in harmony with truly human values. It may imply that your relationships with others go deeper than trying to beat them. That's not to say that competition is bad. Competition is a necessary element of being human. In fact, it's a feature of the larger world. Becoming is the nature of reality, as everything is constantly in the process of pushing and pulling against everything else as it competes through a will to power. Nonetheless, this will to power is predicated on cooperation and the ability to form and reform. Atoms and molecules, and various elements must be able to come together in order for the world to hold together. They must be able to come together to separate and reform. This is competitive and life affirming. The universe hasn't eaten itself. And it never will. The oceans hold the water even as the water seeps into the soil and evaporates into the air. And perhaps, one day, it will hold together as a dark and cold place as all the stars burn out. Or, perhaps, it will change in another direction.

The world holds together just as community allows for successful competition. The NBA is a community. The highly competitive games and the sweat and effort to win, that we see almost every night, is predicated on the cooperation grounding it. If you only care about winning, or only judge yourself in relation to others, then you are missing the complexity of the NBA. The best NBA players all want to win, but they rarely lose their nobility in the process. Sure, everyone loses it from time to time, that's being human, but overall, the stars such as Butler, Lebron, Curry, Giannis, Durant, Tatum, and Kawhi comport themselves with class and dignity. Others walk a thinner line. It can be tricky to hit the right balance. It's foolish to live by the motto: "if you ain't cheating, you ain't trying." At the risk of sounding too Kantian, imagine if everyone adheres to this maxim. The only reason cheating works, sometimes, is because most of us know not to deceive. We understand that if everyone acted subhumanly, we wouldn't have a human world. Therefore, once we enter adulthood we have a duty to repress or sublimate that infantile attitude. For really, are we so shallow and stupid, so competitive and starved for superficial recognition that we can't see what is important, what matters, and can't act as such?

When we can't see the truth in life, we obsess over the frivolous, we fixate on appearances. Why would one want to have a lawn in the desert? Learning to live within the natural environment might aid one in actually dwelling, in connecting to nature and one's place as it truly is, while letting its long-existing processes continue to thrive. Of course, it doesn't follow that we shouldn't leave any mark on the world. We don't have to obsess over our carbon footprint. We are part of the world, and we have the right, as much as anything, and more than most, to exist, and to bring the best of what humans have to offer into the world. Anthropomorphism isn't intrinsically immoral or narcissistic. We cannot not be anthropomorphic any more than a bird can not be a bird. However if our actions create whitewash upon the world in the name of winning, then we are pushing the worst aspects of humanity.

We can assert our will to power into aspects of the world when it makes sense and not do so when it's not rational and not consistent with who we want to be. I don't have to just destroy things because I can, and I don't have to accept that a tornado will destroy me, simply because it could (though my desire to show how brave I am shouldn't drive me to go outside in the middle of a raging storm or chase tornadoes around to feel alive). Further, I probably shouldn't compete too much with my body, either. Listening to one's body can be a source of self-knowledge and can connect one with more than mere ideas of what one might think a body should be like. Our bodies change throughout our whole lives, and much of it we won't like. Ultimately, bodies stop working. Freud tries to remind us, in the third chapter of *Civilization and its Discontents*, that we are connected to the world but that the gadgets and technologies we are creating are causing alienation. I don't have to be lying on my back in the grass, gazing up in the sky, to connect to the environment and to my body. Yet it helps. It's certainly better than staring at my phone while driving. Actually, seeing where we are and feeling what our bodies are doing is a philosophical practice. What if we ignore the ideological noise of the latest fads? Will we get to a deeper place? What's all the buzz attempting to distract us? It's merely surface noise that will fade rather quickly, only to be followed by more cacophony. We aren't missing anything by ignoring it. Knowing that everything is will to power doesn't mean that I have to push my foot all the way down on the gas pedal. I can slow down and, perhaps, see something I would otherwise miss. We could listen instead of chatter; we could pass instead of shoot. Obsessing over winning or believing that life is a competition is to not understand the self nor the human condition. Living is an art.

We must remember though that the irrational drive to compete and win is not simply a product of our society. It's deeper than that. At some points of history, and at some moments of life and Being itself, the drive, and even the need, to win takes the driver's seat. Survival depends on it sometimes, and even non-living material forces interacting will destroy as well as create. As part of the id, the impulse to compete and win, just to compete and win, will always be somewhere inside of us. Still, we can largely learn to control it. Sometimes having the ability to exert human power is not a reason to exert human power. Certainly, the drive to dominate in an infantile manner is part of the human condition. We have all succumbed to this urge on occasion. We all know it. All of us have gone back and apologized for it because we understand it was not right. Thus, we are fighting a two-front battle. The first is within the aspect of the self that is infantile and only knows competition; and the second is against a society that uses competition to distract us from knowing ourselves, prompting us to consume to fill the void. *La vie philosophique* helps us push back by getting us to ask *what* we really want, and *why* we want what we want. Thinking philosophically, we might even ask if it is really us who is wanting and desiring what we think we are wanting and desiring. Or are there other forces? The exterior world is being made worse by contemporary society, and our money-driven culture is making our bodies and minds worse. We should take personally the suffering that comes from our environment and our bodies today. We live in a world that is now overrun by us. Therefore, we need analytic training to see things correctly. This complicates the related, but differing, goals of avoiding suffering and seeking happiness.

Freud says we naturally try to avoid pain and, as naturally, we seek pleasure. As we saw in the previous chapter, by developing our human capacities we discover that happiness trumps mere pleasure and may require some pain. We may need to accept some pain and avoid certain gratifications to be happy. In other words, happiness has a complicated relationship with pleasure and pain. Although happiness is related to the original goal of avoiding pain and seeking pleasure, it is qualitatively different. Again, it's complex. And we all know this, as we all strive to be happy, but also wonder if it's ultimately possible to achieve, let alone sustain. Suppose one wins an NBA championship; for how long does that keep them happy? Not as long as one might suspect.

It is clear that the three sources of suffering can thwart happiness. At the same time they are also the conditions to be happy. Without nature, our bodies, or social relations, there is no happiness. If a rock falls on your head, or you sprain your ankle, or someone punches you, it will hurt and you will not be happy. When the sun shines gently on your face, your body is healthy, and you are surrounded by people you love and who make you laugh, you are happy. We started this chapter with Freud's point that it's other people that cause the most problematic suffering. And he's right. For if the weather is bad and you are not feeling great, but you are surrounded by others in a loving and productive environment, you may be happy. If you have cancer but your relationships are strong, you may be happy. Yet even if you are perfectly healthy, if your relationships are weak, you will probably be unhappy. Simply put, a vital piece of the quest for happiness is not to allow things to become more important than people, and not to use people merely as if they were things. Maturity is worth striving for. To get to the true meaning of this Freudian insight, concerning the confusion between subjects and objects, it will help to go deeper into philosophy.

Subjects & Objects

The fundamental philosophical issue that underlies Freud's discussion of suffering and the quest for happiness involves the fact that we can never escape human subjectivity and, at the same time, we cannot relinquish objectivity either. We understand that the world itself is more formidable than we are, and that some objects and the world have a more enduring onto-logical status than we do. The world exists, we rightfully speculate, whether humans are here or not. Also, every human, every subject, has a body. Thus, every subject is also an object. Nonetheless we cannot really access the external world as it is in itself. We know a world exists outside of our world, we know we have bodies, and we believe that objects exist when we are not around. Still we can't really talk about the world of objects while bracketing ourselves. Our world, and the knowledge of our world, is only comprehen-sible because we are subjects capable of comprehension. We have to use our senses with our minds to experience the world in a human manner. We have to use our minds to even contemplate a world without us in it. There's no getting rid of us to understand the world. At the same time we also wonder to what extent we comprehend versus to what extent we distort the world, objects, and even ourselves.

We seem to be caught in a human trap and so we turn, ambivalently, to each other to make sense of everything, in the manner that children mimic adults and gaze intensely at others to figure out what to do and to know what is going on. Psychologically though, it's not pleasant for adults to give other subjects that much power. Subjects don't always treat other subjects well, so we might want to avoid others. Better to deal with the weather and the external world, as it may drop rain on your head, however it won't hurl insults at you while casting a bucket of water at you. And better to hang out with your dog or cats, as they bring so much joy, despite the fact you have to keep a doggie bag in your pocket or clean the litter every day. Animals just don't cause the same amount or type of anger as people do. We don't blame our dog for eating a sandwich we left out on the counter in quite the way we would blame a roommate for eating our sandwich! Regardless, even when we shut out others, they are in our heads and are inscribed on our bodies. Our ideas, norms, values, clothes, artifacts, etc., have all been shaped by the human world we are part of as well as human history. Finally, it is only with other people that we can truly have discussions and engage in joint projects.

We know that our dog does not have agency in the way that our room-mate has agency. At the same time, in many subtle ways, throughout living, we mix these things up. Despite being complex organisms, we have the tendency to reduce subjects to objects. The cause is, at least, two-fold. First, some people are treated as less than human because they are not considered fully human. Much of modern moral thought has been utilized to expose this. Thus, there's really little excuse for it anymore. I can't be mean to you and honestly claim I mistook you for a rock, a dog, or even a robot or a witch. I can't think you are less than me simply because you grew up in Ohio. Still, it is not surprising that we act this way. We don't start our lives with the value of reciprocity and the understanding of the nature of reality. Thus, the notion of treating people differently than objects is something we learn as we go. Lower creatures never really develop a hard distinction between the two. They operate according to their perspective without reflecting any deeper on it. In this way, we can say it's deeper inside of us to objectify than to see the humanity in others. Second, we may objectify other agents not because of our lower capacities but also because of our higher capacities. Our human capacity to know that others are free agents doesn't mean that we like it. Sometimes the autonomy of others bothers us as we know this gives them a sort of power. Sartre pointed out that it is really only other people who have the ability to shame us. Therefore, we might just want to shame them first. The motto here is: If I can make your life hell, then, perhaps, mine won't be. In this scenario, we know others are full human beings, and yet we treat them as less than human, *exactly* because we know they are *not* less than us. Why would we do this? Is there a sick pleasure in it? Not knowing another has agency might give one a reason to objectify him or her. Nevertheless knowing that others suffer as much as we suffer, love as much as we love, and think as much as we think, and still we treat them as objects, it's worse, *non*?

This is why Freud's emphasis on evolving is so powerful. We have to evolve to see that subjects are not objects, and after that, we must accept that this knowledge also entails that we don't abuse it. People do abuse it though, because people like to win. Hence the necessity of maturity. Maturity is a condition to know that subjects are not objects. It's another level of maturity not to cheat others of their humanity, just because one can get away with it. If winning is our highest value, we will continue to treat others in a dehumanizing and condescending manner and do so in the name of an ideology of success. On the other hand, if we want to live by true standards, if we care about nobility, and if we want to be as human as we can be, we need to prioritize treating others as full subjects by giving people full respect and granting them full responsibility. We must create environments that encourage this sort of comportment. Truly considering others as human agents implies to see, treat, and hold others as responsible for their lives as well as regarding oneself as fully responsible for one's life. This reciprocity allows for a society in which others and ourselves are recognized as agents. To claim some people are more than this and others are less than that is to misconstrue what a subject is. *Au contraire, la vie philosophique* understands this as it starts with the self: I can't expect to be treated as an agent unless I also act as one. If I want to live philosophically, pursue excellence, and be useful I have to act with my full agency and I must be strong. Usefulness requires strength, courage, and proper focus. The practice of *la vie philosophique* focuses on duty to ourselves and those who matter. Our agency only truly exists when we actualize it in reality. Perfect laws and perfect ideas are unachievable in the human realm. There is no external absolute that can define what perfect justice means for beings living in society or in nature. We cannot wait for the world to be perfect to seize our existence. If we do, we will never be free, we will never live truly human lives.

The most important will to power that we have is our individual agency, and it's easy to forget that we have this advantage. No one else can do exactly what you can do. We deny ourselves and others this truth if we succumb to metaphysical notions that demand a world that matches an abstract idea or a metaphysical belief. Nietzsche warned us about projecting into the lives of others.[43] This is a type of arrogance that easily corrupts the higher good and objectifies others in subtle ways. For example, perhaps unknowingly, when we pity others we reduce them to an infantile state. When we pity ourselves we do the same. Today, pity is perceived as a virtue when, in reality, it is a will to power. To pity my fellow mortals, to pity myself, to act as if we are not agents is far from being noble. Additionally, it has become a way of being in the world, a way to feel alive.

Another subtle way that we deny people their full agency is by claiming some of us are more "natural" or more "sacred" than others. If we claim that some people are more connected to the earth or live more naturally than certain others, it may seem like a compliment. Likewise, if we declare that some of us are closer to the gods or connected to something supernatural, it sounds sweet. Yet beneath the seeming admiration of another person or culture lies a denial of their humanity. For neither nature nor the supernatural are standards that humans can aspire to. We already all are 100% natural and 0% supernatural. Thus, buried within the claim of ontological difference (being more natural or being "blessed") is the buried claim that some are not truly human, they are not really agents. If they are more natural, or they live more naturally, then they are not really human like the rest of us. What does it really mean when we call a land or people sacred? Does it mean that some people or places are ontologically of a different substance? Are some of us really witches, devils, and angels living in other realms? When we open this door we find ourselves in a whole new world, a superstitious one. It's a dualistic world: the sacred and the profane. It's a world where

---

[43] For a true critique of pity, see Nietzsche's *Thus Spoke Zarathustra*.

people cannot evolve. Some are magically transformed or blessed; others are not. The former can turn wine into blood and bread into body, or something similar. Like transubstantiation, the claim of sacred people, sacred artifacts, sacred lands, and such, is not a human world. If we *really* thought some land was sacred, would we construct a casino on it?

When we grant land, a place, or a thing unjustified authority, it's another way of confusing the differences between subjects and objects. Above, we considered some ways we objectify others and ourselves, but we can also mistakenly give objects agency. We do this when we treat the world of objects and our environment as if they have free will, as if they are subjects. For example, when Martin Luther thought that a lightning storm was really trying to kill him, he took it personally and convinced himself that a mere thing had subjectivity and agency. I'm sure that we can all relate, that at various points in our lives we have given the things we purchase human or extra-human values or characteristics as though they have agency. Fetishizing an object and giving it motives is another way of living by a false standard.[44] Wearing my Lakers jersey does not help them win. Worshiping a rock will not protect our people. Talking to Alexa doesn't actually give you another friend. Products are sold to us today with the promise of helping make our lives easier. When Facebook was born, it promised us connection with friends and family. While this promise seemed alluring, it also created a lot of chaos among our friends and families. The bizarre thing, though, about fetishizing objects, is that if people believe it works to worship such and such objects, it will have an impact. People will act differently around these things. They will attach special powers to them. How they treat others will change as well depending on whether the others believe that these objects have supernatural force or not. If we decide that you are bad luck, we will start to act differently around you, we will attribute things to you, and you might actually have a tougher time, you might then even start doubting yourself. Perception can begin to create reality. It can get quite complicated. The point here is that it's easy to reify and to fetishize, and these wrong paths can happen at the individual level or at the group level.

Life on Mars

Given the fact that many people are likely to objectify us or value objects above us, it makes sense that many would question whether civilization itself is worth all the trouble. Is it really worth it when we realize that life in

---

[44] Marx famously called it "the fetishism of commodities." See *Capital* (Penguin, 1992) Chapter One.

the civilized world will not run smoothly? Freud understands our impulse to throw in the towel, and he understands the roots of the drive, but he warns us not to give in to the desire. Nothing good awaits us on the other side. Scratching the anti-social itch will only push us back toward the anti-civilizing tendencies of the id. We will turn to the unfiltered pleasure principle and start acting like a spoiled child and start complaining that civilization inhibits our freedom, our choices, and our autonomy. We will start to believe that we would be better off forgoing civilization itself. However, when we do this, we have simply been tricked once again by the id. The id is a master at getting us to forget reality and to forget what is good for us, and what will truly make us happy. In this case, the id gets us to forget that civilization isn't really a choice. It's a condition for becoming human. Precisely, we cannot go back to our childhood, we cannot fruitfully return to some pre-civilization without losing our humanity. First, we were not free or happy in any deep sense prior to civilization. Freedom, choice, and autonomy, as we know them and want them today, are products of a civilization. Outside of civilization all that waits for us is barbarism or anarchy. And we know that when things fall apart, indescribably bad things happen to human beings, more often than not.

Despite Freud's realism, he does occasionally fall into "state of nature" speculation. He considers that we could forgo civilization. And he's right to do so as long as we contemplate it in terms of simply leaving one particular place in favor of another. This drive is deep in the American imagination, given our past of coming from all over the globe. Everyone who has ended up here came here at some point or came from people who came here. Further, given the nature of space and place in themselves, one can always dream of heading toward something promising. Today that includes heading up to Mars. Before we just take off, let's not forget Freud's insights about the dangers of nature and the limitations of our bodies. Traveling into outer space is hard on the body, literally. Moving into a new apartment or house is exhausting enough. We probably are not really built for great upheavals. It's always tempting to scrap everything and try somewhere new when the going gets tough or when one is bored, or has messed up. Either way, baggage seems to follow us whether or not we actually consciously packed anything for the trip. Furthermore, every environment we move to, will, in some fundamental ways, be the same. Everything on earth is impacted by gravity, the sun, etc. We won't find an essentially different place on this planet and we won't find fundamentally different people. Moving from California to Ohio, we will probably be eating at McDonalds as we cross the states. And one day, Mars will probably have a McDonalds too, and a "happy Mars meal." Hence, going to another planet will change some of the details of our lives, but it won't allow us to escape our existence.

Still, it's not completely irrational to want to "occupy Mars." Sometimes the best move is just to leave. In certain circumstances it can be rational to say that you have gotten all you can get from your city, your family, your friends, your job, etc. Of course, given that we are social and tribal animals, it makes life easier when you grow up in a family or community that allows you to flourish. Unfortunately this is not always the case. Alienation is not a pleasant feeling. It can make the quest for happiness seem almost impossible. Still, it's a two-way street when considering alienation. Maybe the place is the problem, maybe it's the individual. Our lives and our existence are different. Our bodies and an environment are necessary for us to live and breathe, but we must seize our existence and give it concrete meaning. This requires both internal and external adaptation. Violent adaptation.

The world itself is a violent place. Creating oneself as an individual, akin to creating a civilization, will be violent. And violence will be necessary to sustain both too. To be an individual requires differentiation. Differentiation is violent. Something or someone is always excluded even when one is being inclusive. Inclusiveness changes what was prior to the inclusion, and it creates destruction both internally and externally. Even if one proposes that we make no distinctions or differentiations, we don't escape the trap of violence. Doing nothing is violent toward that which is harmed by doing nothing. And, even if it were possible, what could be more horrific than replacing all differentiations in favor of making the world into an undifferentiated whole?

The question is not a question of violence or non-violence. It's a question of directionality and being able to give reasons for one's position. It's a question of what sort of violence we are willing to tolerate or not. In the same manner that pleasure does not *a priori* equate to goodness, social values such as inclusion, diversity, freedom, etc., don't *a priori* equate to goodness either. Inclusion and diversity that are rational and coherent in a specific situation are good; otherwise they are not. Instead of arguing over abstract labels and ideologies, instead of thinking that because these things are social constructions we have some *a priori* knowledge about them or have some essential control over them, we need to look at all of them in context, and ask if the reasons for supporting or not supporting them are valid. It is necessary to do so with a sense of modesty and openness. It's easy to trick the self into believing that one's own positions or ideas are rational and moral. How about we listen and think, as much as we speak? We know that much of what is new in life turns out to be wrong or misguided. We should be wary of the intuition for panacea solutions.

It's wrong to fetishize any group, individual, concept, or idea. We don't need to think that expecting others to give reasons is somehow intrinsically oppressive. We don't need to think that the outside perspective will never be given a fair shake. Our modern history refutes this. If outside perspectives were always crushed, nothing would have changed, ever. To assume, beforehand, an insurmountable bias or even a bias, negatively conceived, is a metaphysical claim, an arrogant and cynical perspective, and a will to power. To say another might be wrong does not prove they are wrong. To say that we cannot say, with absolute certainty, that Steph Curry is the best three-point shooter in the NBA is not to say that discussing who's the best shooter is completely relative or unknowable. Further, it doesn't follow that other types of players will just be ignored, underappreciated, or disrespected if we start from the premise that Curry seems to be the best. To disprove the claim that Steph Curry is the best shooter requires presenting a stronger argument that shows that there is actually another player better than him. Until there is, and unless one articulates it coherently, we have the right and duty to grant him his greatness. Likewise, to simply say that someone *could* become a better shooter than Steph Curry does not prove that someone will become a better shooter. Maybe someone will or maybe not. Sorting out good reasons from bad reasons is not always an easy task. Still, when Curry scores, the truth is being proved.

The Warriors (but not Golden State)

Freud warns us that there is no easy path to happiness, and that no utopian ideas, or radical ones for that matter, will succeed in producing a happy society or individual. Today the world is still full of ideologies that preach the opposite, and full of individuals, who use civilization, to create careers out of bashing civilization. Freud asks, "How has it happened that so many people have come to take up this strange attitude of hostility to civilization?"[45] Looking around today, one might conclude that people are cynical and stupid. Additionally, when there's money to be made and groups willing to be manipulated, this attitude will arise. To this Freud says: "I believe that the basis of it was a deep and long-standing dissatisfaction with the then existing state of civilization and that on that basis a condemnation of it was built up, occasioned by certain specific historical events."[46]

---

[45] *Civilization and its Discontents*, p. 58.
[46] Ibid., p. 58-59.

This is interesting. We usually think of Freud as trying to explain things at a scientific and biological level. He mentions "the victory of Christendom over the heathen religions. For it was very closely related to the low estimation put upon earthly life by the Christian doctrine."[47] Did Freud secretly read more Nietzsche than he admitted to? Now, we know, Freud was as honest as anyone, meaning not very honest, but we don't have to go crazy over it.[48] If Freud did draw from Nietzsche, he could have done worse. Nietzsche gives a description of everything we have been talking about here that is philosophically acute and more entertaining than almost anything else we will read in philosophy. Appealing to some formal categorical imperative cannot match a mythic story of warriors, priests, and the downcast. The moral law within my head gives way to the aesthetic taste in my mouth. It's worth turning briefly to Nietzsche, as he goes deeper and further back to flush out the philosophical point that Freud is gesturing toward in his claim that the hostility toward civilization is to be explained genealogically.

In *On the Genealogy of Morality* Nietzsche says, with tongue somewhat in cheek, that it all started with a powerful group's infighting.[49] The Nietzschean story is one of a quasi-mythic society of warriors. These warriors were especially strong and built for that particular environment. It naturally suited them, and from that base they developed an ideology and a morality consistent with what they did and how they lived. They attached a story to it. A story that, of course, made them the good guys. The inhabitants judged themselves by this standard. They judged others by it too, even those they were close to. They would have had, as we say in philosophy, both a descriptive and normative conception of what is good and who they are. What allowed them to thrive they would intuitively believe was good and right. They would see themselves as blessed and invent gods reflecting their values. They would see those they dominate as losers or weaklings. It wasn't a moral term, it was just that life is a competition, and the warriors would see themselves as winners since their world (descriptively and normatively) validated them. They would say "it's only natural that lions eat sheep."

At some point though, some of the strong would stop being strong. Sometimes an individual loses his or her edge and sometimes it takes a generation of two. In any case, those who lost the warrior ability would try, for as long as possible, to stay in that class. When they lose their physical edge, they might scheme to hold on to a life of power. Without the right body, they turn to the mind, and create a job for themselves such that they still appear

---

[47] Ibid., p. 59.
[48] As Frederick Crews seems to have.
[49] See Nietzsche, *The Genealogy of Morality* (Hackett, 1998), First Treatise.

essential. They might have given themselves priest-like titles (or PhDs) to justify their places with the winners. They can't physically keep up with the true warriors, so they tell a story rationalizing it. They invent an identity for themselves. "We are the Priests!" They say it's not that they cannot keep up, it's that they choose not to. They assert that they are actually higher than and more pure than mere warriors. They start to see the original values (physical strength, courage, etc.) of the warriors as not good, instead of admitting it's just something they can no longer thrive through. They pretend that they choose a life of abstinence and un-adventure. The priests, perhaps, start to believe their own story and, in any case, they realize the warriors won't buy this forever. The warriors will see, at some point, that they don't need the priests. So the priests turn to the oppressed in the society and convince them that their oppression is not justified. This gives the priests power, recognition, and a massive congregation to serve them. They use big abstract words, as that's the only weapon they can now wield. They basically tell their new flock that their situation is merely a social construction. The warriors have tricked everyone and secretly hid the others spiritual superiority, their true selves. Since the oppressed have no positive identity themselves, they begin to obsess over the warriors, and they over-interpret and misinterpret (with the encouragement of the priests) the actions and motives of the warriors. In effect, both the priests and the oppressed are full of fear and resentment, so they interpret the warriors as more than simply unreflective and selfish brutes, and conceive of themselves as more than just unfortunate and unlucky.

This is the beginning of a transformation of values that includes a new essentialist definition of "free will." An essentialist notion of free will allows people to believe they can magically transform their life conditions through their beliefs and thoughts. Mistakenly believing one has a special object inside the self, one that unproblematically triggers agency, is both to reify part of the self and fetishize a human power. It allows one to disregard subtlety and complexity in favor of a Manichean worldview. This prompts the others to believe they are truly the warriors. There is no need to analyze their own talents or qualities, let alone test their skills. The ideology teaches them that it's not that the warriors are naturally strong and suited for that world, rather it's that the warriors have consciously and maliciously created the society just to humiliate the wretched. It's basically a conspiracy theory. Enter essentialist thinking. The transformation from good versus bad to Good versus Evil is now possible. While the strong define themselves by what they actually do, the weak define themselves only in contrast to the strong. They look for features and attributes that are merely different as opposed to higher and relevant. My red hair is more than red hair. It's a sign, a sign of my fiery powers. And I must believe that your lack of respect for my red hair is a moral failing and a choice you are making with malicious intent. This misconception gives me permission to hate you, judge you, and punish you. Now, I can think myself grand, as I have the moral courage to accentuate my red hair and identity as truly a Redhead. I am to be celebrated and congratulated for my bravery in really being me. If one has an ideological perspective such as that, it makes it easy to interpret the warriors as Evil. When one starts thinking in essentialist terms, facts, history, and reality lose their meaning and give way to interpretations that would not be coherent without the metaphysics. If I believe in the devil, so to speak, my interpretive powers become magical, and truth and reality disappear. Those who lost their ability to be warriors, and those born into unfortunate circumstances, now have the ability to give themselves a heroic story.

The warriors, of course, saw themselves as good and those they defeated as worse than them. A championship basketball team sees and knows they are champions. They see those they dominated as not as good as them. This is not judgmental, it's not moral or metaphysical. They just want to win and to be the best. It's based on reality and it stems from a vision of what's higher. Excellent basketball is recognizable in form and content. Winning basketball is higher than losing basketball. There's nothing metaphysical in the original ideological, moral, or existential structure of the warriors. Unlike the warriors, the priests and their followers must concoct a fiction, an origin tale, and a mythic heroic story, to give their lives meaning.

These latter sorts of identities are essentialist and metaphysical. They take the form of "I really am X." Since this X is not actualized, one must be told or taught that it exists. The X is in a place one cannot see. The idea of having a true self inside oneself, something, I know not what, takes form through the teachings. This creates an ideology of "we are all special just by being us." What does this mean? It means that rather than pursuing genealogical or hermeneutic understanding we start to attach labels to what were once simply actions one does in a life. When life has no concrete meaning, this is what people do. Banal things take on a new significance. Instead of simply saying: "Sometimes Tom plays basketball," we start elevating it to "Tom is a basketball player." This claim precedes whether I actually make it to the NBA or not. It's based on my wants, beliefs, ideas, and feeling alone. And if I don't make it, it must be someone else's fault. Even if I make it, that doesn't completely satiate me. The next step is, "I have a true self that is, above and beyond everything else, a basketball player." Now, if you deny me my identity anywhere and everywhere I go, you are evil, for it's something essential about me. It does not matter whether I'm on the court or not, I'm a basketball player everywhere including inside myself. I even start to worry about what you call me or how you label me when you are not talking directly to me. This manner of viewing the self is problematic enough in itself, but it becomes insidious when it is not directed toward noble activities.

At some points in history, some people were told they were sinners, or something akin to that. Perhaps they were told that their oceanic feeling reveals their truly perfect selves. In any case, many believed it and it caught on. Rather than encouraging people to evolve and become free individuals, and rather than aiding them in becoming healthier and stronger, we created labels and institutions that solidified them as sinners or something. The result, ultimately, was fundamental change in human society that created people with incoherent identities, problematic needs, and empowered institutions grounded in irrationality and a resentment toward this world. Of course, irrational solutions may seem like a cure. Giving drug addicts their drugs keeps them happy. It keeps the drug pushers rich and in power. Everybody feels good and righteous. Still, regardless of what some people believe and others say, in reality, there are no sinners in the world. Nonetheless, we continue to validate untrue beliefs, turn them into identities, and alter institutions. In this way, we are still medieval.

Chapter 4 — Love & Labor

> After primal man had discovered that it lay in his own hands, literally, to improve his lot on earth by working, it cannot have been a matter of indifference to him whether another man worked with or against him. The other man acquired the value for him of a fellow-worker, with whom it was useful to live together.[50] — Sigmund Freud

Freud starts Chapter Four reminding us of our prehistory. Humans needed to labor collectively to evolve into civilized beings. Just as individuals develop through stages, our ability to labor changes over time and this allows for new possibilities, for both individuals and civilization. We have the ability to keep improving, both quantitatively and qualitatively. We don't survive by mere instinct like some other creatures. We have to channel our instincts into human history. Considering, as soon as we realized that it literally takes our own hands to survive and to enhance life, we would not be apathetic about others who are either working with or against us to secure our material conditions. Work is good for us and we know it deep in our bones. Waking up in the morning with something productive to do aids us to want to get up. Besides, when we work with others, the work itself is intensified and our relationships deepen. The character of individuals emerges through their work. There's nothing wrong with expecting people to work hard and assessing them by how well they work with others. In the context of work, one's ability to labor is the true standard. This truth is deep in our history and prehistory. As Freud points out, work matters for our survival and it matters for our character. He was convinced that holding

---

[50] *Civilization and its Discontents*, p. 77.

a job is one of the central pillars in building a happy and good life. Freud's motto is: Work is good for you. Work.

From Work to the Jumbotron

Similar to Freud, Marx understands that our labor changes over time and that it is connected to the quest for happiness and higher values. In the *1844 Paris Manuscripts*, Marx details how social labor builds human beings into civilized creatures.[51] For when social beings labor, it is done collectively, it builds from the past, and it is loaded with norms and intertwined with linguistic practices. In our capitalist system, one can see both the dehumanizing aspects of social labor and the liberating elements. Capitalism comes along at various points of history, perhaps *en media res*, where labor is capable of producing adequate surplus. One needs capital to have capitalism and one needs surplus to sell on the marketplace. Aside from natural surplus, labor must have evolved enough that humans can make things rather efficiently and it requires that we are treating each other somewhat as agents. This can be interpreted in class categories of workers and owners. The workers, in theory, are free to take their labor where they wish. Owners are given the right to control the residual. We understand that a capitalist system has liberating and progressive elements when contrasted with some other economic systems and the "state of nature." There are norms and linguistic practices in a capitalist system that promote morality, individual and collective responsibility, social interaction, and so on. Of course, not all the values are progressive and some will promote false standards and distort reality and manipulate justice. Still, if human beings are interacting in a capitalist system, then civilization has progressed in objective ways and has institutionalized norms that promote certain human values. Nonetheless, capitalism falls short in helping us develop beyond market values and it continues to alienate those within the workforce.

Marx isolates four types of alienation in capitalist labor, yet he also recognizes that they all blend into each other in interesting ways.[52] The first aspect is alienation from the product itself. At one level, the product that one is creating is an alien force that dictates what we do and how we do it. To some extent this is rational and necessary, as the material properties of the object can only be altered based on its true properties. If I'm working with a liquid, I will need to keep that liquid in something solid. Or if the object is large, I need an adequate work area. If the thing is alive and needs

---

[51] Marx, *Economic and Philosophic Manuscripts of 1844*, the Marx-Engels Reader (New York: Norton, 1978).
[52] Ibid., See pp: 68-111.

sunlight, I may be working outside. However, these conditions don't alienate me from the object so much as show that it's independence as an entity in the world. I may help make the thing, but I don't control it completely. Neither does anyone else. Even so, if, as a worker, I have no control over the product, except as I'm told I must interact with it, then I will experience alienation. Since as a mere worker I don't own the product nor control it, the product stands outside me. Not being able to truly put myself into the object and not being able to see myself reflected in my work is true alienation. As a worker, I am separated from something I should not be disconnected from, I am being treated without dignity or full agency. Under these conditions, I cannot fully participate in my work and so my actual life, in these moments, suffers. When your work is robotic, when labor is boring, it's hard to care about something that you are only interacting with because you need the wage. Furthermore, when one's freedom, in relation to the work, is limited for irrational reasons, labor will be alienating too. In a capitalist system the workers may have more or less freedom concerning things they interact with than in other systems. It really depends on the specific situation, though we can imagine that a better society would allow workers greater possibilities concerning objects and in terms of their environment generally. Analyzing work from a true standard means treating workers as the free agents they are, and seeing the product as the object it really is. A truly good system would create environments suited to useful and excellent labor.

In this regard, Marx would point out that it's even more consistent with truth when we see that most objects exist because of the social or human labor that created them. Our laboring today comes out of a tradition and is predicated on the labor of the others who preceded us. When we look around us and see all the objects in our world, we recognize they did not just appear magically. Human beings created virtually all of them. This links us to the past and to others. In this way, objects and products show us our human power and should invoke the value of gratitude for those who work now, as well as those who labored before us, as their work allows us to labor better. Objects, when seen truly, show us the social processes that literally put that object into existence. It connects us with our traditions. Labor should be a reflection and a concrete example of our human will to power, both as individuals and, more truly, as a historical collective. It's not just relevant from the workers' side. The owners, who have deeper responsibilities, also have trouble, in a capitalist system, appreciating the deeper truth of the objects that surround us. Owners face alienation from products, as their relationship to the products is one of trying to gain profit from it. In a capitalist system, the owner cannot be too fixated on the true material properties of the product nor on the socially useful aspects of the product. Still, regardless of where our focus is, the use-value and the social processes that allowed for construction create an artifact's value. When one understands this, and can interact with the object and the world in accordance with this knowledge, one will be greater. People will see their individual lives as part of the species life. It should invoke in us a sense of duty and gratitude. This points to ways that civilization could continue to evolve according to true standards of value.

The second aspect of alienation stems from the historical activity itself. Again, in a capitalist society, we see we are *en media res*, as laboring activity is better than in some previous systems but it is not even close, about halfway, to being fully human activity. A worker's activity under the logic of capitalism is not artistic, free, ethical, or deeply meaningful. Rather, the worker is simply part of an apparatus generated and perpetuated for profit. Anything and everything else is secondary. The same holds for the owner's activity. In our system, one must think in terms of power and profit. One must act and be cunning.

The final two types of alienation are: alienation of individuals from each other and from the recognition of one's species. These are just two sides of the same coin. Human labor is social, both literally and normatively speaking. Workers compete with other workers for jobs and they compete with owners for pay, retirement benefits, etc. In addition, owners too compete with other owners and they work to replace human labor with non-sentient alternatives. The alienation may be quite a bit less than in other times. Even so, there are layers and layers of conflict in this system. Some of them are apparent every day. Rather than producing a world that values its cooperation with others and rather than working to redeem the promise of our species, capitalism puts us in a world of competition and individualism. It attempts to be an ahistorical schema such that we relate to the world through rudderless commodities and for the satisfaction of egotistical self-interest and id instincts. It does not tap into our higher aspects of being human and it does not aim for truth and understanding. It alienates us from each other and from our species as a whole.

Marx's analysis supports Freud's claim that labor is fundamental to civilization. It is one of the pillars of why we even have civilization and it has to be structured well enough and fair enough, otherwise people will revolt or opt out as soon as they are able to. It's not irrational that people in society expect labor to be decent. It's not unjust if they are resentful when others do not work. People have a right to criticize those who are not carrying their fair load. The roots of how we feel about labor run as deep, perhaps deeper, than human civilization itself. Marx's analysis also supports Freud's insight that labor is essential to human character. Our values, our attributes, and our characteristics show themselves in what we do and how we do it. Our laboring practices are a power that impact our language and our beliefs. In this way labor is embedded into all spheres of the superstructure, and when labor is irrational and unfair, it will need rationalizations and justifications to sustain itself. Capitalism runs partly on propaganda; it distorts our notions of the values of freedom, equality, and happiness. Modernity is an intriguing place, as it is complex enough to harbor both the deepest sources of suffering and the richest possibilities for happiness.

According to Freud, civilization started with labor and love. He describes the parents of civilization as Eros and Ananke (Love and Necessity).[53] He paints a picture of these fundamental elements emerging out of a worse condition, a condition in which others are under the tutelage of a pre-civilized and dominant father figure. It's a world of terror. It takes courage and intelligence to overthrow the tyrant father and to create a collective system. Freud imagines our origin as a band of brothers working together for something beyond individual self-interest and above pre-civilized instincts. In this way, civilization also ushers in justice. Justice is not a given, rather it is something we must create as we discover what's true and possible. Those who, like the tyrant father, see only self-interest, pleasure, and unfiltered instinct, are not civil, and we cannot have a good world if they have power. The subhuman represents a world without justice, an id world, that is egotistic, and consumption based. It is a world that doesn't understand the true value of labor.

Civilization requires that we work and that we work collectively. This, according to Freud, means that labor will never be completely satisfying. Unlike the tyrant father who takes everything he wants, in civilized society individuals cannot and should not have all their wants, needs, and desires satisfied. Civilized labor means compromise. It's an infantile fantasy to think labor should be perfect. Still, the idea that labor can and should improve over time, and make us better, is both a Freudian and Marxist idea. We don't need to give up the quest to keep our labor evolving. In fact, social labor that gives individuals a certain amount of freedom is one of the pillars of modernity. Today's freedom is often overstated and ideological, but nonetheless, there is flexibility in our system. We should have the freedom to compete for a job and to leave a job if it doesn't suit us. This process needs to be fair and transparent. We should have the opportunity to start a business if we have the desire and resources to do so. When work is structured rationally

---

[53] *Civilization and its Discontents*, p. 80.

and justly, it can give people dignity and power. The power one gains from labor should be appropriate to his or her role in work. With some types of labor and at some levels of the laboring process, different degrees of power are appropriate.

A point guard has a different role on a basketball team than a center. The point guard needs to bring the ball up the court and has certain responsibilities for running the offense. The guard has power that others don't have. To determine the justness of this, one must understand the position, the player in the position, and the philosophy of the offense. Players who are role players and players who don't typically get in the game still labor and have duties. They might get paid less than a star point guard but they also deal with less responsibility. The coach has his or her role too. Some of the necessary attributes of a great coach extend to almost any coach and some will be particular to the individual and the vision of the team. Coaches need to be able to adapt to different players and situations. In this way basketball is a complex laboring system with room for freedom and pretty much every sort of person. Teams and players value others as they contribute to the success, and this is why keeping the true standard as the motor driving the industry is vital. Players don't have to be friends off the court or know things about each other not connected to the job as teammates. It's not unusual for NBA players to switch teams in the middle of a season. It's remarkable how quickly these traded players connect with the team. It's also not remarkable, because the players and coaches value each other for the right reasons.

Today, basketball is big business. There's a fine line in our society when it comes to sports and capitalism. For the major sports, excellence still matters. People are not completely willing to sacrifice excellence yet. At the same time in professional basketball there are also a lot of other things going on; there are multifarious forces impacting the direction the game is taking, as well as everything it's connected to. The ability of players to shoot the three-point shot today, and the rules and normative changes that allow for it to be such a weapon, give basketball a different flavor. This changes who can make it to the top. There's a change in the skills of the players and a change in the game. It impacts how and what kids practice and mimic. While Steph Curry gets credit for being the catalyst for the change, it's no accident that this style is better suited for a television product and an uneducated basketball public. In this way, one could suggest that the changes are not completely positive. As basketball takes on a certain popularity and connection with various mass cultural ideologies, it is impacted and it impacts our world.

Basketball, on the court and in the culture reflects our society and helps shape it. On the court there is a hedging of the norms and of what's appropriate. In our society there's a loosening of the lines of what's appropriate. It's astonishing how reckless many drivers are on the highways and roads. Many of us will get into auto accidents and some will even die on the roads of America today. Driving is meant to help make our lives better. It takes cooperation on the road so we can all get where we need to be safely. Sadly, the focus is not on being a good and considerate driver but on competition and image. Many hide behind the wheel while steering with their id. We even insist on the "freedom" not to have cameras punishing those who burn through red lights. In basketball today we don't blow the whistle when one takes too many steps (we simply rename it "Euro-step"). Further, it's perfectly acceptable to carry the ball, palm it, and jump into the defense to draw a foul (although they are working on that one). And let's not even get into the calls and advantages that the star players receive. To be fair, some of the changes are rational and make the game better. That's modernity; it's a mixed bag of the good, the bad, the fun, and the ugly.

Laboring activity can get better over time and there are ways to improve anything. However, when changes are made to make the game more sellable, people must have their guard up. If anyone can understand the activity without investing some time and care into learning about it, then it's just a spectacle. If we have to be entertained every second, there's something really wrong with the event and with us. At NBA games they give people no space to relax, reflect, slow down, or interact with others in a truly human way. Every second that we are in the arena there is distraction and entertainment, and, of course, a constant pressure to consume. When we are walking around, televisions are every ten feet, robotic music is constantly blasting, venders are screaming, prizes can be won through an app on the phone, and everyone shuffles around like zombies looking for more blood. People have been so conditioned and so overstimulated that it's reached the tipping point as they constantly demand more. It's changing the human essence. Heads are becoming softer than nerf basketballs, and language is reduced to rhythmic lullabies. We can see the smirk of the tyrant father mouthing, "I'm back!"

When a toy has broken and spins faster and faster in a circle, everyone fixates on it although its movement is meaningless. At the game, everyone is looking but no one is going anywhere or seeing anything. Every timeout, entertainers run onto the court and shoot useless junk into the stands. At halftime the spectacle formula is put to use with some bizarre circus act at half court, or they bring some fans forward for a distracting contest. It's all bread and circuses. And it's too overwhelming to ignore. The hope that one day one will get on the court and chuck the ball from half court, or run the court against another poor stiff, solidifies, in the mind, the idea that in

America everyone has an equal chance to be a winner (but only if we are willing to run around like chickens with our heads cut off). All the time, this "challenge" is being displayed on the big screen above. People are continually teased that they might get their 15 seconds of fame, constantly looking up on the big screen hoping to see their own image. Somehow seeing one's face on a mega screen prompts some to enact as children at a birthday party. The jumbotron is the idol that centers this religion and ensures we are living in 1984. Did we trade the tragedy of the human condition for lottery pics?

A consumer society combined with an entertainment society is not a good society. Consuming and being entertained should be very limited activities, for the true value of them is only in intermittent distraction. In very small doses they are rational and healthy. Of course, everyone needs to relax. *La détente est nécessaire.* Unfortunately, today we are driven by cultures that fixate on constant fun and distraction. Mass culture is weirdly infantile and salacious at the same time. Horkheimer and Adorno observed this long ago: "Works of art are ascetic and shameless; the culture industry is pornographic and prudish."[54] Sex and animal comportment have been slipped into every sphere. Even intellectuals cannot see, literally cannot see, what they are being shown when they watch a film such as *Mignonnes.*[55] We blame our problems on the past, on everyone else, and on everything except the harm we are actually doing to ourselves and others through our consumer culture. This is a very touchy subject even though it is difficult to deny what really drives our mass culture. To think that today's record labels, producers, and commercial artists are in the business of preserving authentic culture or growing beauty is dubious. To believe that these capital crusaders are in any substantive manner able to produce beauty through their cacophony is tantamount to believing that books generated by Chatgpt continue the tradition of *writers* with living mastery of language, felt sensuality, and true understanding of the human condition.

A society that values meaningful work would not be a consumer society and would not spend the bulk of its time on entertainment and competition. Freud's writing on work makes it clear how necessary rational labor is to civilization and to the self. Rather than the current attractions, we need to focus on building a world through and for truly useful work. With a scarcity of noble labor, the trend in the youth today is not to want to work.[56] They desire to have more leisure time. It's understandable that young people

---

[54] Horkheimer and Adorno, *Dialectic of Enlightenment* (Stanford University Press, 2002), p. 111.

[55] See Louise Perry, *The Case Against the Sexual Revolution* (Polity, 2022), pp. 59-62.

[56] At the moment, the consciousness of today's labor being problematic seems greater in France than in the U.S.A.

don't want to work in our society. At the same time the idea that constant relaxation will be rewarding, or that we will be living better simply if we have more free time, is fallacious and hedonistic. In a problematic society, the leisure possibilities will also be problematic. They may even be more problematic as, at least with labor, one might be creating and building something tangible and useful while interacting with the object of labor. Further, one hopes that the labor is developing at least some worthwhile human skills. Today's so-called leisure is structured as work and controlled by industry, laced with *faux* interaction and useless skills. Leisure is an historical construction that does not simply allow us to do what we want whenever we want to. Modernity's empty values dictate what leisure means today. We both overemphasize and underemphasize the idea of free time, as secretly it is nothing but a tool for capital. In a good society, when one works and has leisure after, it elevates the self. It grows the person and provides kindling to burn steady and with beauty. If we work constantly, we burn out. If we play continuously, we burn out too. Leisure could be a chance to grow our individuality, reflect on one's life, and develop one's unique qualities, capabilities, and virtuosity. Sadly, the colonization runs too deep for a noble *détente* to even be meaningfully understood today. Leisure today means free time to consume and be entertained. As such, one's wants, and even needs, are created through the society and for the society. But it's also deeper than that.

Hardish Determinism

Contemplating the manipulation of our desires and our free time leads into a deeper philosophical puzzle. If our needs, wants, impulses, and actions come from a prior place, how do we even know if we have free will? It is often argued that Freudian theory is deterministic. The idea that everything that happens in the world runs via necessity is an ancient idea. It's both a philosophical and a religious one. The idea of Fate, or of a God that sets the table, so to speak, for all that will happen is deep in the human imagination. In terms of philosophy, the idea is more ancient than Socrates and we see different articulations in pre-Socratic theorists such as Leucippus and Democritus. Democritus even posited the sophisticated theory that everything in the world is composed of atoms in motion; the idea that the world is a material becoming is not a new fad. It goes back thousands of years. Despite its coherence, it took quite a while for Democritus's idea to catch on. This should be a lesson to us that truth is not always an easy sell. If we are living in a society with an untrue schema guiding us, truth can remain concealed for a long time. In this case, it took until around the time of Newton for another sophisticated determinism to be seriously revealed again. Moreover, at this time, thinkers such as D'Holbach, who anticipated Freud, claimed that as much as there is necessity in the physical world, there is necessity in our brains since our brains are also material things. Thoughts directly come from the brain, thus thoughts are not free. They are analogous to flower buds forming from out of a stem. The flower doesn't choose what or when to bloom. Finally, around the same time, Pierre Laplace linked these scientific and philosophical ideas with spiritual ones when he introduced what came to be known as "Laplace's Demon." He imagined a being with complete scientific knowledge. If such a being could grasp all that was going on at a single moment in the universe, it could then predict, with absolute certainty, the future. In other words, in principle everything happens because it has to happen.

We are children of all this speculation. Our religious, scientific, and philosophical front loading has made us so we have supernatural intuitions, cause and effect reasoning, and a deep sense that we are free, all floating inside our minds. This trinity does not live together in perfect harmony, and Freud has his method of sorting it all out. To understand Freud's articulation of determinism, it helps to begin with modern philosophy's way of talking about determinism. Within contemporary philosophy Freud is sometimes referred to as belonging to the school of "hard determinism."[57] Determinism is the view that claims, if the world works according to cause and effect and unfolds through linear time, it is impossible to have free will. The first two parts may seem intuitive. We think of the world as operating according to causal laws and we experience the world as unfolding in time. When we ask questions of why things happen, we look for prior causes that are responsible for the event. This can be stated as: "X caused Y." The idea here is that if X happens, then Y will happen. For example: why am I here today? Because my parents wanted a child. The parents "causing" or creating a child results in there being a child. X causes Y, and X explains the existence of Y. I didn't choose to be born, it wasn't a result of my free will. This is clear. The philosophy of determinism goes a step farther by claiming that if I didn't choose to be born, nothing I did after my birth truly originated from me. Thus, I do not have free will. The present moment in which I'm living is *completely* determined from the past.

Let's look more closely at the final part of the claim of hard determinism. This is where things get interesting. The hard determinist says that when one event necessitates that another event will follow, freedom is not possible. It's the prior event that is responsible. When we try to find a moment of

---

[57] This is sometimes called "incompatibilism."

freedom, we are forced to keep going back in time to something prior. We never find an event responsible for itself. Humans came upon the scene at a certain point of the world's unfolding, suggesting that everything we do was determined by what came before us. Simply put: if X happens, then Y has to happen. There's nothing and no one that can change this schema. If that's the case, then the event or thing had to happen, and freedom has nothing to do with it. The hard determinist moves from this common sense view that certain events are not free to showing that this actually proves that no events are free. Any and all Y only happened because there was an X that made it happen. And the X had to happen because of Z that came before the X. The hard determinist claims that everything in the world is completely subject to the laws of cause and effect, implying that everything that happens has to happen, and everything that doesn't happen couldn't have happened. What came before determines, in a hard sense, what comes after. According to deterministic logic, I had to write *this*. Sorry.

Freud's metaphor of the Eternal City, present in Chapter One of *Civilization and its Discontents*, can be interpreted as deterministic. He illustrates how we can trace the layers and changes of a city to what happened in the past. In the same manner we can trace the layers and changes of an individual to what happened in his or her past. The world has been unfolding for ages before our birth. When we enter it, we are clueless to what is going on.

We are pushed and pulled by forces greater than us, which develop in us habits, perspectives, needs, wants, and instincts without us even choosing them. What's in us comes from the larger world. We are simply slotted into the universe. Similar to a long amusement park water slide that we were put on, we are flying down the slope without any personal control, and we will crash when the world decides, when the slide ends, and not when we want it to end. It may look as if we have some control, as our arms and legs are flailing about, but in reality this is much ado about nothing. In other words, regarding the important things, such as the true direction of our lives, our character, and our actions, Freud claims that we play little to no role in determining them. The world and our inner world are the Z and the X to which we are the Y. Since who we are comes out of the past, meaning itself is deferred or unclear, as the past is cloudy and deep. It is a backward moving Eternal City.

In other writings Freud affords this story more details.[58] By around the age of five our personality and directionality are formed. We didn't play any substantive role in shaping our personality, traits, attributes, or character-

---

[58] Freud, *Three Essays on the Theory of Sexuality* (Verso, 2017), *The Interpretation of Dreams* (Basic Books, 2010).

istics when younger, and we couldn't have. Our character is forged before we even know we have a character. Later, after we get older, we still are driven by forces that run deeper than us. Freud emphasizes biological triggers, childhood trauma, and all the fantasies our id has been stirring up from the start. Our ability to fantasize and process fear, love, desire, and needs is not a conscious or controllable ability. Additionally, there are the world's forces, forces mostly unknown to us, yet pulling us in every direction. From nature's laws to society's expectations we are constantly bombarded from all sides. We resemble a raft floating in the pacific ocean during the middle of World War II.

In Freudian jargon, our possibility for freedom would come from the ego guiding us rationally and consciously. However, the ego is trapped between the id and superego (and a cultural superego). Any of those alone would probably be too powerful to fight off, but together they present a rather insurmountable challenge to any robust conception or possibility of freedom. Freudian theory then seems to present a rather pessimistic picture of us. Not only are we determined, but since we don't feel determined or truly believe we are determined, we are unwell. We are all sick because we can't face reality directly and honestly. Even when I make an effort to be conscious, to be rational, and make free choices I'm probably really being directed by forces tricking me. If what I believe and want today can be traced back to what happened in the past, then what I want and believe today are not things that I freely chose. Worse yet, even if I could show that my choices were not determined by the past, I'm still unwell and not free. For if my wants and beliefs of today do not come out of a past, and do not have a structure to them, then they are simply random beliefs and wants. A leaf being blown in every direction by the wind is not more free than an eight ball being shot into a corner pocket by a professional pool player. Life's a trap: if my actions come out of the past I'm not controlling them, and if my actions do not come out of the past then I'm not in control either. When we think about our own lives, we realize how little time we are actually consciously making decisions anyway. Most of life just has to be lived, and too much thinking gets in the way. Further, how many times have we really thought things through only to realize later that we made a bad decision or that our reasoning wasn't based on what we initially thought it was? Freedom is not fleeting on this account, rather it's impossible in any robust sense. One can understand why some seem to be programmed zombies controlled by jumbotrons and LCD screens they cannot look away from. If this is the case, the whole quest for a life as a free and happy individual seems doomed.

Fortunately, for those interested in *la vie philosophique*, Freud's vision is not quite this dark. I suggested that Freud was a "hard determinist," but his theory is a bit more sophisticated than a scientific view that fetishizes cause and effect. Freud, as philosopher, proposes a theory that leaves room for some freedom. However, it takes work and commitment to seize one's freedom. One must want to evolve, put in the work, and get the proper help. There's an old joke: How many psychoanalysts does it take to change a light bulb? Only one, but the light bulb has to want to change. Technically though, because we are not light bulbs, we don't change. We have a nature that begs for growth. If we don't evolve, we crystallize, turn into light bulbs — empty inside but shiny on the outside. Freud's promise of happiness depends on us wanting to evolve and mature. At the same time it recognizes how difficult it is to succeed. The first step is to want to evolve. The second might be in recognizing the moments where we have exerted our freedom because we have all had experiences in which we have used our consciousness, our ego's rationality, our will power, figured things out and acted accordingly. We've all, at one point or another, reasoned well, and pushed our will into the world in such a manner that we have changed the course or direction in which things were going. We do this with little things and, sometimes, with bigger things. Of course, Freud would warn us that when it comes to important things in life, it will be much harder not to be directed by unconscious drives and infantile experiences. At the same time, it will be easy to underestimate the power of social forces. Nevertheless, that's part of the art of living. Freud's theory of happiness requires that we work.

Work is not only to gain money or to earn a living but also to grow a self. We have to work on ourselves. In today's world we like to talk in this language, but how many of us really work on ourselves? It's not something one can just do on a weekend retreat. It's a day-to-day and slow process that very few have the courage to take on. It requires focus, reflection, and the ability to build habits based on knowledge of one's qualities and capabilities. And this knowledge must be hermeneutically coherent with the world. It must fit with true standards of making oneself useful and aiming for excellence. To avoid the discontent of living in civilization, to fend off this malaise, will demand a complete paradigm change. To truly grow, requires not just choosing one or two things differently, rather it means adopting whole new values, goals, and standards, and being willing to live concretely by them. In this way, changing one thing requires altering one's whole life, and giving up all the infantile pleasures our society worships. It's no wonder that Freud is not popular today.

In reality, Freud is a soft determinist. While hard determinism denies that freedom is possible at all, soft determinism just recognizes that freedom is difficult and requires work. We will be controlled in life unless we evolve and seize our freedom. Hard determinism makes the mistake of treating the whole world in a narrowly scientific manner. It interprets everything in the universe, or reduces everything, to planets revolving around the sun. This school of thought places cause and effect in the center, making it the new God. The words "cause and effect" are human constructs. It's part of our way of understanding reality, and it is undeniably pretty consistent with how part of the world works. Still, the phenomenon we call cause and effect is subject to other forces in the world. Cause and effect itself is situational. In different contexts it has different powers, and in some contexts (including, it seems, the microlevel in physics) it plays no role at all. Cause and effect are simply pieces within the larger laws of nature. Causality itself is predicated on and relational with multifarious forces, which brings us back to contextual intelligence. For Freud, it means that people are responsible in certain situations. He understands that it's evolutionary. Perhaps free will is a result of evolution, and it came into being at some point, and to some degree, in each of us. In some individuals maybe it only flickers from time to time; in others, perhaps, it is robust. As individuals with the ability to evolve, some will evolve out of and away from being determined. Precisely, we all evolve out of needing to wear diapers, and some evolve to be able to read philosophy, some to hit a three-point shot, etc. Free will, perhaps, is a species and individual quality subject to evolution. Those who seize their freedom become more free and those who refuse to acknowledge their freedom lose it.

Or, perhaps, as a species, we all have free will in us and it's up to individuals to choose whether and when to utilize it or not. Perhaps it's similar to our ability to smell: some things we cannot help but smell and other things require focus and care to smell. Further, we can work and develop our sense of smell and make distinctions that were impossible for us before. Likewise, sometimes we might just choose freely, and other times, we have to focus and care to choose freely. Maybe it takes work and time to develop or, perhaps, it's simple to tap into. If the past makes the future, maybe it made our future free. Perhaps we are comparable to certain species of birds that all have wings today, even if that species didn't in the past. Perhaps the past caused a qualitative change, as when an artist takes an object and transforms it and puts it in another environment that completely changes its character, capabilities, and meaning. Maybe a determined past unintentionally created a free future. Clearly, some people do learn to seize their freedom; some learn to flap their wings strong enough to fly. Gaining knowledge of why we do what we do is part of getting on the road to freedom. We become, and if we are clever, we become free in even deeper ways. Perhaps one needs a pinch of luck too. Many things in life are driven by our pasts, and many are not driven by it. Maybe I'm playing basketball today to get ready for my game tomorrow. Playing today is driven by the future, more so than the past. Sometimes one plays basketball solely because it's fun. It's not always intelligible to locate the meaning of why one does what one does in some dark, deep, and myste-rious past. Maybe I'm in the mood for basketball because I wrote all day and my body wants to move. That's an explanation that appeals to the past in an innocuous way. It's rational and consistent with freedom. I could have chosen various ways to exercise but I chose something I enjoy and something consistent with the vision of my life. It is something that links me to others I care about and have a history with. Of course, one could simply say I'm still trying to prove to my middle school coach that I should be the starting point guard. Nonetheless, that interpretation is not as coherent as the former.

As adults, we have reason. We have the ability to do things for reasons that are worthwhile. I could let the past control me or I could be bigger and stronger than that. Freud believes that weak people let the past control them, that they allow the false standards to seduce them. Once we know the truth we should live by it. Again, it gets back to rationality, habits, and will power. If my reasons for doing something make sense and go beyond simply reacting to something in my childhood or some silly social pressure, then maybe it's a good reason, and hence, maybe I freely chose it. When we give reasons and they don't make sense within the context of our lives, then we are probably being driven by something irrational, from the past or a social pressure. It's not about whether our reasons are a social construction, or whether they come from the past, rather it's about whether they make sense of the situa-tion and make sense within our lives.

Those who identify as hard determinists might claim that their true selves know that they have no control and no freedom. This is fine. Live and let live. However, we could ask the question as to whether this claim is coherent or merely imaginative. In other words, is it really relevant to our actual existence and for our social interactions? If people claim certain rights or privileges based on a belief, we could accommodate them so long as it doesn't spoil the meaning of our social environments, and so long as it's fair to everyone. People can believe what they want. We all have ideas about ourselves that others don't understand. If I do my job while bracketing the parts of myself not relevant to the job, no one should care. In fact, they don't necessarily need to know. We should ask ourselves why it's important for others to know certain things about us. What's really going on? The art of self-deception is a constant battle, *non?* My philosophy students don't need to know I play basketball, whom I vote for, what foods I eat, what shows I watch, what I do on Saturdays and Sundays, what happened in my child-hood, if I'm married, where I vacation, etc. Someone could be a determinist and not let it interfere with his or her job or, when it's relevant, only then bring it in. But mostly, no one needs to know, and no one probably cares, if one identifies as a determinist so long as everyone does what's required in the context of our interactions. In most, and maybe all, social situations, it doesn't matter. There's a whole world of determinists running around today. There are different groups of soft and hard determinists, and some prefer to be called compatibilists or incompatibilists. All these labels have no bearing on our interactions.

It becomes problematic if I think my identity as a hard, or even a soft, determinist means I can teach philosophy without a philosophy degree. In this case, wouldn't you be right to deny me? It's not fair for people to iden-tify (let alone teach) as philosophers if they haven't spent the time learning, studying, and living the tradition of philosophy. However, if I have a philos-ophy degree it might actually be nice for the students to have an incompati-bilist as a teacher, although, really, one has no concrete idea why that would matter or what it would mean. No two individuals, even those who are both hard determinists, are that much alike that they would be interchangeable. Turning individuals into such an abstraction or a sign is an unworthy way to treat people. Still, we can treat individuals as individuals and let them label themselves pretty much as each desires, so long as we don't violate true standards.

For example, we could extend the definition of a hard determinist to those who are not determined but think they are, or even to those who wish to be determined but aren't. We could proclaim that anyone is free to be a determinist if it suits his or her fancy. In other words, anyone could live freely as a determinist. Logic isn't everything. Certain identities are not serious enough for it to matter. For example, strictly speaking, only a person with paranormal powers is a witch. Still we could extend the identity of a witch to include those without paranormal powers. We could call many different people witches, including: those who think they are witches and those who wish they were witches. We could even extend the definition further and call everyone witches, if we so desire.

Another approach would be to dissolve the category and say, "you are not a witch, because no one is a witch." When it comes to identities, we can ask if they are coherent, rational, and relevant. People might decide they are hardworking, honest, sensitive, etc., because they rely on astrological birth to define themselves. One might say, "I'm a Capricorn, thus I'm hard working, honest, and sensitive." However, rather than pretending that people have essential identities, or pretending that identities somehow exist outside and beyond concrete contextual situations, we might just say that some individuals, and groups, think these things are important. Some people might carry their hard determinism into every sphere of the world and every potential sphere of their lives. I may believe that being a hard determinist is what's allowing me to drive my car with great skill rather than understanding the actual talents that make me a good driver. In reality, of course, the former doesn't make one a competent driver, and it is silly to think that it does. Still, lots of beliefs are silly. It's not any worse or different than thinking God is always watching us or believing some people are witches or believing that the devil is around every corner or believing in Astrological signs. *Hélas*, it's also not any better.

Determined to Love

Freud understood the complexity of the human imagination. Philosophical puzzles such as determinism, considered in the proper contexts, can help us evolve and grow. We can and should have spaces in which to test and experiment with new puzzles and identities. Regardless, we need to continue to grow our highest and most noble qualities for living truly human lives. Freud would remind us that we must keep our labor and love central to our lives if we want to develop our greatest human capacities. If labor and love are not guided by our highest and most noble qualities and capabilities, no other contexts or identities will matter. Without labor and love we will not grow our virtuosity. If we forgo these deeper things, we have fallen back into false standards of power, wealth, and success. Sadly, our lives will not be useful or excellent. We will not be living a philosophical life. Putting into practice *la vie philosophique* requires concrete labor and concrete love. These matter, as Freud emphasizes, for our survival and for our character. If society allows other things to supersede, surpass, or illegitimate meaningful labor and true love, that society will not be useful, excellent, or splendid. Yet it might think itself getting closer to perfection.

Today more people believe in perfection than believe in determinism. The common sense view is that we are free, plain and simple. However, philosophically, Freud seems to be on the side of the stronger argument. Part of the reason there is pushback against Freudian determinism is because of our pre-philosophical past and the belief that humans are both natural and supernatural. Many ideologies argue that we are the creatures in the universe that are at the same time part of the world and not just part of the world. Many critics of Freudian theory stem from a standpoint of dualism. In some religions it takes the form of believing in a soul that stands opposed to the body as an essentially different substance. The idea here is that the soul is spiritual and not dependent on the material world. Descartes's dualism is part of this tradition and, as such, gives the view deeper philosophical legitimacy. For Descartes says the mind is the soul and is a spiritual "substance," while our bodies are mere replaceable, material cogs in God's machine. The soul gives us free will and makes our essence perfect.

Humans often look for quick and easy answers to life. Of course, when living our lives some of the complexity must be bracketed or ignored. Our perspective cannot take in everything. Thus, we almost naturally make false judgments more than one would hope. We think we have a soul that triggers free will because it is, in one sense, a simple and straightforward answer that has been bequeathed to us. We extend this faith to the self, thinking of it as a simple and straightforward thing, that is until we read Freud. After that, can we ever look at ourselves in the mirror quite the same way? As Freud puts it: "there is nothing of which we are more certain than the feeling of our self, or our own ego. This ego appears to us as something autonomous and unitary, marked off distinctly from everything else."[59] At the same time, he points out that this is deceptive and that "the ego is continued inwards, without any sharp delimitation, into an unconscious mental entity."[60] We are each one being, even though there are layers and layers to us. Descartes was wrong. We are not dualistic beings harboring two essentially different substances. Rather, as birds developed wings, we developed consciousness and free will. It comes from our evolving in a world that allowed this all to be created. Through living on this planet, we developed reason, consciousness, and freedom. With this freedom some concluded that we are ontologically special, with eternal souls from another place, and others concluded that the idea of free will is a fiction. Such is the human condition.

The same goes for love. The world did not have love until we created it and chose it. Akin to a mad scientist we mixed id energy with rationality and practicality, and then threw in a dash of spicy-superego, and *voilà*, love was born. Through shared labor and couples love, we built civilization. Today we deny love. We are partly right to do so. We are not free when we fall in love, but it is not merely determined outside of us either. It comes to us and on us. Still, we are free to build it or not. It takes work to keep it, as with anything worthwhile. It can turn pathological as at "the height of being in love the

---

[59] *Civilization and its Discontents*, p. 26.
[60] Ibid.

boundary between ego and object threatens to melt away. Against all the evidence of his senses, a man who is in love declares that 'I' and 'you' are one, and is prepared to behave as if it were a fact."[61]

Romantic love is the strongest bonding agent for civilization. For love makes us crazy and strong and motivated and noble. It gives us a reason to settle down. It gives us regular sex, but it quickly becomes more than that. Deep companionship with another we love pushes us into a human realm. Discussions, shared interests, children, and building and dwelling together become as important as carnal satisfaction. Without the love element, civilization has no chance. Labor alone is not sufficient to prompt the risk of being around others. When people connect in a physical, intellectual, and practical way, and dwell together, it turns into a spiritual connection. It makes it worth risking more than what's narrowly rational, and it provides deeper roots for humanity. It gives us something worth dying for. Yes, of course, it can turn into the opposite. Of course, it can exacerbate hate and violence. Love has the power of a gun that can protect or harm. Love makes men willing to die for women, and vice versa. Love of one's children makes women willing to tolerate all kinds of things. It can be messy, but with love and those willing to work, we have the roots for building something excellent. Love and labor are linked directly to Freud's earlier discussion of the centrality of pain and pleasure in the human condition. Work is necessary to alleviate suffering. Through labor we make our lives better; while love and sexual fulfillment gave us the highest pleasures and became a prototype of all happiness. Still, both labor and love are not guarantees of happiness. *Hélas!*

Love and sexual attraction are much more mysterious than almost anything else. When love fails, it causes more suffering than when work relationships fail. The true quest for happiness needs love, and love is the one thing that can also guarantee we will not be happy, as it can cause the deepest suffering. Love can turn bad in many ways. First, I might be rejected by the one I love. Second, I may find love only to later have it spoiled, if I betray my beloved or vice versa. Third, death can take away forever the one I love. Because of all this, and more, "wise men of every age"[62] have cautioned us not to pursue love. Regardless, it seems most of us are not free to not seek it. Very few can live a rich and happy human life without love. If one is fortunate, one can find love and it can provide more pleasure than pain, and it can sustain a life and make one happy. Some people won't risk it or have had bad experiences, so they put love into an identity, God, some tribe, or Humanity. Freud disagrees with this *naïveté*. Not everything is worthy of love; not everyone is

---

[61] Ibid.
[62] Ibid., p. 81.

deserving of love; not everyone is lovable. Love is not something you give to everyone. To think everyone merits love is to be seduced by a false standard. Even so, since so much of our being is at stake when we truly love, we deny this truth, unless we are determined not to.

CHAPTER 5 — TRUE LOVE, TRUE AGGRESSION

> So far, we can quite well imagine a cultural community consisting of double individuals like this, who, libidinally satisfied in themselves, are connected with one another through the bonds of command work and common interests. If this were so, civilization would not have to withdraw any energy from sexuality.[63] — Sigmund Freud

Civilization can be a frustrating place. When we don't get what we need, or even what we want, there will be consequences. Freud sees that sexual frustration is one of the most difficult to process and we understand this when we read about individuals who have lashed out in society. Many young male terrorists speak of sexual frustration and the alienation they experience in the world today. People become neurotic when they cannot tolerate their lives. They often turn to intoxicating substances and substitutive satisfactions such as drugs, alcohol, internet addiction, identity politics, and supernaturalism. This will further damage the individual's mind and body, as well as make it more difficult to function and be happy in concrete or actual reality.

Double Individuals

Change is difficult. It's often said that people can't change, and although we don't like to admit it, it's true. People don't change. We can evolve, and we should. Still, it takes work, reflection, luck, and willpower. As Freud sees it, the difficulty of cultural development is linked to the "inertia of the libido,

---

[63] *Civilization and its Discontents*, p. 90.

to its disinclination to give up an old position for a new one."[64] It's almost impossible to redirect the inertia into a noble existence unless we are in a virtuous environment and are surrounded by the right people. Sometimes it only takes one other person to get us to move in the right direction. In fact, ideally it will be only with one other. Depth is more important than breadth. Love in its highest form is vital to a good life. It's in capturing that another is unique and irreplaceable that we become fully human. We want this one and not that one, and they want us. Attraction is specific. Sexual attraction and the energy, the will to life it puts into a self, is exactly how Aristophanes explains it in Plato's *Symposium*.[65] When we fall in love, we feel invincible, godlike, and we don't need food, sleep, or anything else in that initial period. It can build into a relationship of companionship and true subject–subject interaction. Freud, as well as Aristophanes, praises the power of two becoming one. Freud calls people in love "double individuals,"[66] and he imagines that if only we could build a society filled with double individuals then civilization wouldn't have all the problems it has. For the sexual energy would be distributed rationally through reality; each would be "libidinally satisfied in themselves"[67] and "connected with one another through the bonds of common work and common interests. If this were so, civilization would not have to withdraw any energy from sexuality."[68] Finding the right person and being the right person is not easy. It can take time, and the timing for the two must fortuitously coincide.

Given the makeup of our bodies and the human psyche, true love is only between two individuals. True love is intense. Capturing particularity requires concentration and focus, as in a very intimate gathering aimed at what's distinct. More than two creates the problem of dilution on one side and perversion on the other. It creates a problem of jealousy on one side and indifference on the other. As Freud puts it, "sexual love is a relationship between two individuals in which a third can only be superfluous or disturbing."[69] Our bodies only become complete with one other; multitasking doesn't work, especially concerning relationships. Focusing directly on the other is vital to know him or her, as well as to show your partner that you are serious. Who likes talking to someone when they are constantly checking their phone for who knows what? True love requires a certain sort of particularized understanding, loving maturity, and devo-

---

[64] Ibid., p. 89.
[65] Plato, *Symposium* (Hackett, 1989).
[66] *Civilization and its Discontents*, p. 90.
[67] Ibid.
[68] Ibid.
[69] Ibid., 89.

tion that our consumer society detests and rejects. Two people in love don't need things. They are happy to love and to be loved. They don't have to buy anything, but our world tries to convince them they do. It markets love as it markets automobiles. The result, in America, is that people love their cars. They fetishize them and treat them like agents. Just watch a car commercial and you will understand. The anti-human love marketing machine today has turned into a binary trend that socializes the youth with either "you don't need anyone" or "don't limit yourself to just one other person." Both of these choices are only appropriate for subhumans. It's a perversion of what is best in us, and neither is a true standard of excellence. Of course we need others. Why would saying "I don't need anyone else" or "I won't change for anyone" be interpreted as anything but sad? It's not empowering. Further, having sexual relations with more than one person is just a symptom of an imma-ture, bored, confused, and manipulated person.

In Aristophanes' telling of the story of love, of the "double individual," he self-consciously makes it comical, imaginative, and extraordinary. He too understands that love is the necessary ingredient of a true civilization and an indispensable brick for a worthwhile individual life. As he puts it concerning Eros: "of all the gods he is the best friend of men, the helper and the healer of the ills which are the great impediment to the happiness of the race."[70] His myth is an origin myth, like so many, that imagines that somewhere in our past our ancestors were stronger and greater than we are today. Our ancestors were almost godlike. Such fictions, which is to say all accounts of a past that posit a greater, more free, gentler being that we have somehow lost sight of, set out to explain what happened that made us so wretched today. There seems to always be a bad guy. According to Aristophanes the villain was Zeus. Still, we somewhat asked for it. We were originally double beings with four arms and four legs. As our bodies were quite different than we are today, our nature, our attributes, and our capabilities were different also. Primal man "could walk upright as men now do, backwards or forwards as he pleased, and he could also roll over and over at a great pace, turning on his four hands and four feet, eight in all, like tumblers going over and over with their legs in the air; this was when he wanted to run fast."[71] We were complete, whole, and powerful. So powerful, in fact, that we could venture toward Mount Olympus and try to reach the summit. The gods knew our intention was to lay "hands upon the gods."[72] We had a desire for power and for a godlike existence. This is understandable as we are mortal, and there's

---

[70] Plato, *The Symposium*. Project Gutenberg, Retrieved April, 9, 2023, from https://www.gutenberg.org/files/1600/1600-h/1600-h.htm.

[71] Ibid.

[72] Ibid.

no great joy in that. *Ce n'est pas la joie!* If we could become king of the castle, if we could occupy the land of the gods, then maybe we could live forever, not suffer like humans suffer, and find happiness. This explanation for why people venture to new lands risking their futures and lives is more plausible than many of today's accepted accounts. Aristophanes knew his story was a story, but we may not be able to say the same for much of what passes for narration today.

Aristophanes wasn't afraid of truth, so his story has complexity to it. He tells us that our ancestors were a bit mischievous. We were zooming around and the gods felt threatened. The relationship was a bit ambivalent as the gods liked that we honored them with sacrifices, but our threatening behavior made them question whether it was worth it. What material benefit does a god receive from a human sacrifice? Of course, it's flattering and something to brag about, but not worth getting overrun by. One can always find new worshipers. Nevertheless, that's risky too. Who are today's worshipers, whom are they worshiping, and why exactly do they admire those whom they do? How many identities today would dissolve away if there were not others gazing in one's direction? How many identities would be interesting if there were not, at least perceived others, against them? What would there really be to talk about? In the case of the ancient and petulant gods, it seems that their life would lose some substantial meaning without idolizers. What does that say about them?

In any case, the gods did not want to give up the advantages of having us around, and Zeus came up with a brilliant plan. Rather than destroy us, he decided we just needed to be taught a lesson. Further, as gods have vulnerabilities too, he needed to protect his people. If we got to the top, who knows what would have happened. Thus, Zeus stopped short of the nuclear option of destroying us, and he merely split us in two, using his thunderbolt. This had the effect of preventing us from taking over the universe, and it changed our nature. We are broken and vulnerable human beings who need to evolve to become whole. The split did bring some value with it. It knocked some of the hubris out of us. As we became less godlike we were able to evolve and develop qualities of compassion, fear, vulnerability, patience, and many more. Rather than unreflectively pushing onto the world, we learned to live with other beings and in harmony with the environment. Our id was tamed. Still, from time to time, we try to run roughshod over everything; old habits persist. We discovered how central love is to our existence. How often do we recognize truth when we lose something? How much do we grow after a loss as compared to a win? Our morality, our need for others, the importance of knowing oneself, the truth that gods are not to be trusted, etc., came along after we were cut in half. After this split the quest to find true happiness grows wings. We want to be whole. This doesn't mean that we want to go back to our infantile, hubris oriented selves; the true slogan is not "make America whole again." No, we shouldn't want to regress and go backwards. We should want to evolve into a human whole.

And to be whole we need civilization. Eros gives birth to humans in a place that requires that we have other virtues to survive and to thrive. The virtues are connected. We don't have rational labor unless we have planning and order. Labor must be orderly to be built, and it must match the order of the world. We don't have love if we don't have cleanliness. One doesn't necessarily smell oneself, but others smell us.[73] If we don't keep clean we are not respecting others, and we certainly are not capable of love. Beauty is what makes the quest worthwhile, as it allows us to see into the good in the world and ourselves. As the promise of happiness, beauty only is disclosed fully to those who are complete. All the foundational virtues matter, and we won't be complete unless they are connected. These virtues, these higher goods, are vital for civilization, and if we don't learn our lesson and get it right this time there will be worse consequences than the first time. Zeus may split us again: "continue insolent and will not be quiet, I will split them again and they shall hop about on a single leg."[74] Or perhaps this has already happened and we don't know it. Have we been split again? Do we merely hop around on one leg, with half a brain, and half of human virtue? Do we live in accordance with the true standards of love, labor, cleanliness, order, and beauty, or have we become pogo sticks jumping up every second so we don't miss what's going on in our mindless world? Have we stopped believing in love, stopped looking for it? Pascal said humans are thinking reeds,[75] but have we fetishized our bodies, objectified our minds, and become unbridled weeds choking out the cultivated plants?

Plato, Aristophanes, and Freud understood how difficult it is to put all the pieces together. Love itself can almost seem impossible. What are the chances that I will find my other half? And even if I do, it could be too late. As we live, we change our form. Perhaps we evolve into something better. We cultivate order, cleanliness, and beauty into an existence of hard work. Perhaps our other half does none of this. Then a fit, that was once a fit, no longer matches. We are beings in time as well as space. A human life unfolds and is only coherent temporally, and in terms of the stages of human exis-

---

[73] See *Civilization and its Discontents*, pp. 67-75.

[74] Plato, *The Symposium*. Project Gutenberg, Retrieved April, 9, 2023, from https://www.gutenberg.org/files/1600/1600-h/1600-h.htm.

[75] Pascal, *Pensées* (1646). Also, see Project Gutenberg, https://www.gutenberg.org/files/18269/18269-h/18269-h.htm.

tence. When one lives in a death-defying society, in a culture that is adolescent, it's difficult to get into a rhythm of living according to truth. Underdeveloped people tend to hook up with other underdeveloped people. Sometimes in a bad relationship there are no victims. Violent people and ambitious people often find each other. Sometimes two people do the same bad things to each other. Lots of people think life is a race to get to the top of Mount Olympus, and they treat others like the kid's game king of the mountain, pretending it's okay to push everyone else away, choosing to run up a polluted hill and then feigning hurt and ignorance when someone bigger and stronger pushes them down. Sometimes two people are both at fault. Maybe both are not treating each other or themselves as moral agents. Maybe both are playing a game and acting immaturely. Maybe that's the hidden meaning in the words "me too."

True love between two individuals makes them complete. They don't compete. They need no one else. Still, we are beings that exist through time, and there comes a time to have a child. Civilization needs lots of people, and people age, so they need others to take care of them. The double individual cannot sustain itself. Having a child becomes a rational expansion of love. Still, reality is complex and a child contaminates, so to speak, the initial relationship, and threatens it. Civilization too pushes for the family to grow, even as its growth will threaten loyalty to civilization. Family interests generally take priority over other interests of civilization. Thus, civilization creates ideologies telling us to love everyone, from our neighbors to strangers, and even sometimes to our enemies.[76] Civilization has to sell itself as the family is content in itself. The former must convince us to fight for our country and spread our loyalty. This is somewhat irrational for individuals, but, at the same time, individuals need civilization. As we enter more and more into society, new needs and wants come along. In society we develop friendships. Some friendships naturally cultivate desires for intimacy that threaten the original family pairing. This challenges true love and complicates civilization. It must be artfully lived through. It can't be eliminated. Love has a possessive element, and mixing the family with civilization will bring out jealousy and aggression. War, both internal and external, grows with every step in civilization. Aggression is fundamental to civilization, as there will be competition for many things, but especially for sex and love. What we love, others will love too. We employ both religion and politics in an attempt to manage all this. Let's first look at the religious path.

---

[76] See *Civilization and its Discontents*, Chapter Five.

Religious Love & Freudian Religion

Freud says the maxim "love your neighbor as yourself" is older than Christianity but that Christianity solidified it into the Western tradition.[77] The prescription to love one's neighbor follows from belief in a perfect God. We have seen that the very idea of perfection is contentious and leads to new problems even as it seemingly solves others. For example, in the previous chapter, we briefly noted that the idea of Fate or a God that knows all, complicates the intelligibility of free will. If one is free to make a decision, it seems that this decision couldn't have already been written by Fate. Our understanding of time prompts us to think that if God knows what we will do before we do it, then we might not really have free will. Philosophers and theologians have come up with clever ways to think around this. Belief in God also problematizes the problem of evil. For if God is perfect, and that perfection includes being all-good, then the problem of the origin of evil arises. Where did evil come from if God created everything? And why does God allow for evil when God could prevent evil? Freud is adamant that the world is full of evil, that aggression is omnipresent. He doesn't trust his neighbor, let alone strangers. He has a real problem with the notion of loving one's neighbor, and he's almost at a loss for words when he contemplates loving one's enemies.[78] Still, the idea of a perfect God may motivate the conclusion that we should love everyone. God wants us to love everyone. We are all God's creatures. We are all children of God. We are all brothers and sisters. Freud sees this ideology as civilization's way of trying to reduce some of the natural aggression and violence internal to having a society. Further, because we cannot trust civilization, we develop a belief in God to protect us both from nature and from others, as well as to help control our own instincts.

We saw earlier that Freud locates the origin of the oceanic feeling in the unconscious id, and he sees religion as developing from and through it. We also saw that Freud's theory entails that the human mind preserves something from all stages of the past. Some of this is consciously accessible. I can remember what I did this morning and yesterday, and I can easily access many things from my past. I can use photos or talk to relatives and friends and continue to recount much that I forgot. I may be quite surprised with some of the memories I can draw back up into consciousness. To make life tolerable, we may have an evolutionary bias to remember innocuous memories from our past. We often remember things incorrectly. This helps us cope with reality. Complicating this, as our biology is fragile, we need to be able to remember certain negative experiences. We are inclined to remember

[77] Ibid., p. 91.
[78] Ibid., p. 93.

certain things that have hurt us in order to avoid being hurt again. In this way, trauma shouldn't necessarily be thought of as bad. Being impacted by certain events and experiences, and keeping this in awareness, might be interpreted in a positive light. Today we act as if it's always a negative to have had unpleasant experiences. This is silly. We grow from tough experiences; it can be quite helpful to be in environments that make us uncomfortable. There's nothing *a priori* wrong with feeling stress and being uncomfortable. You could just ask yourself: Is my life in danger? If not, then why not try to understand how this experience would be good? Why not inquire as to why you are uncomfortable? It may help you grow. It might build true resiliency and maturity. Would it make sense for someone trying to develop a strong body not to lift heavy weights under the pretext of not wanting to feel uncomfortable or stressed? Being under stress, uncomfortable and hurting, is a condition to grow muscles. It's a condition to evolve and not something to be feared or always avoided. In a society that teaches instant gratification and perfection, not everyone understands the virtue of letting oneself be uncomfortable and letting oneself make mistakes. Any uncomfortable pressure gets labeled as trauma. *Il ne faut pas faire une tempête dans un verre d'eau.*

Strong negative experiences, and the ability to remember them the correct way, aid in our growth, survival, and future good life. Consciousness needs to be attuned to both the good and the bad. We need to have the ability to recall positive memories as well as the negative ones. If I want to be able to function well, I need to be able to reproduce the positive that happened to me in order to diminish the negative and to put it into perspective. It's a Stoic technique to remind us of how fortunate we are. For most of us, our lives are pretty good. We are alive. We have the skills and time to read this. Still, life is complex and we sometimes fixate on the one negative word someone said, or the one bad experience we had that day, and it clouds everything else. When we let this happen we are blocking out the greater reality. Still, here's where it gets tricky: it's one thing to remember the good so you don't lose perspective on life; it's another thing to remember the good at the expense of reality or to avoid facing your life. It's not wise to escape into a pleasant past memory simply in order not to come to terms with important painful experiences. It may be necessary to bracket certain painful experiences, in some circumstances, in order to function in other contexts. Still, to evolve into greater health, we must come to terms with the past. If the negative is simply being repressed and not dealt with, it might still be controlling us. We need to live artfully so that we don't overestimate or underestimate the extent to which the past dominates us. We need to deal with the parts of our past that are inhibiting our happiness and freedom, and we need to just let go of, or simply move on from, certain things if they are not true obstacles to our thriving.

To aid in this, the Christian tradition emphasizes forgiveness, and this is important. If we can forgive ourselves and others for certain behaviors in the past, we can be healthier and freer. On the other hand, sometimes forgiveness, or the quest for forgiveness, is a waste of time and a distraction from living. The ancient Greeks often stressed *forgetting* rather than forgiving. Sometimes the best therapy is to forge beyond the past. Let certain things go; live in such a way that we will forget certain things. We can evolve beyond them. When we can forget, we give ourselves the freedom to move on without dwelling on those who hurt us. Forgiving can sometimes put people into a cycle of dependency with those they think they need to forgive. Forgetting breaks that link. Forgetting doesn't have to mean completely not knowing about it. It can mean that you are no longer impacted by it. Things happen to everyone. Some things shouldn't be taken personally. Yes, this happened, but maybe it's not appropriate or useful to look for forgiveness. Perhaps I need to just let it go. Forget it. Forget about it. Again, this does not need to mean literally forgetting. By reinterpreting the experience into another whole, I may find it humorous, simply a life lesson, or so insignificant that it has no more impact on me than remembering what shirt I wore yesterday. Yes, I might remember what shirt I wore yesterday, but it means nothing to my life today. That's rational forgetting.

While I am stressing forgiveness and forgetting as routes to happiness and thriving, Freud would caution us here and remind us of the complications of the unconscious. Freudian theory takes things deeper than an individual's life. Many traumatic things from childhood will get repressed as will infantile wishes, memories, and a host of experiences. At the same time, Freud thinks we need to go deeper into the past, not just of our individual lives but into the past of the species and the world itself. The world is *becoming* and what is today comes from what was yesterday, and what was yesterday comes from what was before that, and so on. The new things grow out of the old, and some of the old stays in the new. In this way, Freud can speak of unconscious memories of the beginnings of civilization and even pre-civilization. He's willing to contemplate the very origins of living matter as possible "memories." We can go further than Freud and speak of the possibility of memories or traces of inorganic life, as the nature of reality itself is a becoming, and what was living matter came from prior nonliving matter.

Freud addresses the logic of this, as we saw, in his analogy of the Eternal City. At first glance this analogy seems limited in illuminating Freud's psychoanalytic theory of the mind. In the city analogy, building a new city means destroying the old one. Some pieces of the old city get buried while the rest lies shattered and fragmented and, like Humpty Dumpty, unable to be put fully together again. Still, as we have argued throughout this work, that's not exactly correct. What is old might be preserved despite being seemingly destroyed. What seems new may not be new and might not be whole. What is new might be fragmented. Therefore, one cannot assume that putting oneself back together again means only fixing the past. A positive past can be an advantage or a disadvantage. The present must be constructed well and combined well, regardless of the past. The present is always tricky because we are too close to it to see clearly. What is known today might be a regression of what we once knew. *Reality becomes*, as Lukács[79] put it, though this becoming is not linear and doesn't simply create new things. Sometimes the becoming preserves the past as a whole. Sometimes we just repeat the past, yet think we have moved beyond it. To evolve rationally we ourselves must destroy some parts of the past, and we ourselves must build with certain parts of the past. This is literal. We do not need to construct a new temple by constantly bringing in new bricks from afar. Rather we can destroy a temple and erect a new one using the same bricks from the temple previously there.[80] There are always bricks right under our feet. It doesn't follow that dismantling a "temple" destroyed it or the past. Maybe it's making the past stronger. Maybe we are exactly the same, but cannot see it. Maybe the past is present, but disguised with new words and dressed in new garb. Maybe we are barbarians wearing progressive t-shirts with clever sayings pressed on our chest thanks to cheap labor. Not only are the old "bricks" not destroyed in this scenario, but their external "face" might actually get preserved, as the new builders turn the bricks around to hide the prior symbols, symbols now believed to be antiquated. This makes them invisible to the naked eye, but also inadvertently protects them. The enemies of the old cannot see that they still exist. Nature and the elements cannot get to them. The new society forgets they still exist. We think we have transcended them. Meanwhile it's the new temple's icons, which are perverted, weak, and shallow, that are celebrated, only because they are shiny and seemingly new.

In all cases, whatever is built is built from something and is somewhere. It's almost certain that whatever it is one is working on and wherever one is, there is the trace of the human from the start. Try to find a place on the planet not impacted by humans. We impact everything from the air and soil quality, to the ocean levels and sanitation, to the temperature of the planet.

---

[79] See Lukács, Georg, *History and Class Consciousness* (MIT, 1972) for a complete and true theory of becoming.
[80] See Nietzsche, *Genealogy of Morality* (Hackett, 1998), *Twilight of the Idols* (Hackett, 1997).

Our individual pasts and the pasts of others haunt us all. This is the real ghost story. There are no spirits or supernatural elements at all in this story. Even so the past haunts us all, regardless of what we identify with. We may dig up something about our ancestors' past in which they were wronged, exploited, and oppressed and not be bothered at all. We may harbor no resentment toward the perpetrators, may feel no guilt that our people were too weak to fight back, and may even choose not to identify with them at all. Or, we may come to find out that our ancestors were aggressors and dominators, and we may be riddled with guilt. Freud understands there are layers upon layers, and there's no simple way to predict what will impact us or how it will impact us. There's no simple answer to what exactly we are reacting against or building from. Maybe we think we are angry because of something in someone else's past, and maybe we imagine our life would be better if those things hadn't happened. But maybe we are really angry about something completely different, but we don't have enough self-awareness to understand the truth. Maybe we do know the cause is something anterior, but we are fixated on the posterior. Maybe we do know something's more complicated than we are admitting, but we are shallow and base, and using it as a will to power. In any case, we will either build our lives, or not. Identifications are slippery. Material reality, not so much. The oldest and deepest bricks of civilization are still the foundation and the necessary conditions for human existence today. Meanwhile, today's cardboard temples and plastic constructions, secured with identity glue, left on their own, won't stay upright for more than a day.

Bricks may remain hidden for a long time. Earlier stages of the human mind may sink down to the bottom of our oceanic selves. When some of it tries to come up, we might go ahead and sink it again. Repression exists. What the conscious mind thinks is gone might actually be there. When we start exploring our past, our values, and our norms it's unclear what we will find. Nietzsche[81] warns us about the fate of our idols when we start tapping on them. We realize that many are hollow, while others are a gold mine. Freud has faith that the need for excavation is proper. We will realize that the human past was brutal and realize the necessity of preserving civilization and protecting love as a pillar of it. We will recognize that the brutality can easily return. Only love can prevent barbarism. The double individuals are the basis for later types of Eros relationships in civilization. From the initial love of one other being, we extended our deep feelings to others, starting with children. Maybe one of the two, or both, want a child. Or maybe these double individuals love each other so intensively that they don't need or

---

[81] Nietzsche, *Twilight of the Idols* (Hackett, 1997).

want a child. Their love is complete. Still, unbeknownst to them, or perhaps, despite their intentions, they will have children. If not, life will not go on. These types of situations seem to validate the Freudian insight that more is going on in us and through us than we can consciously grasp. Do we always know if and why we want a child? Does anyone truly know where the desire comes from? This is how the unconscious runs deeper than an individual's past. Schopenhauer locates this will to life outside of agents. Freud's theory is motivated by what's inside of us. What's inside of us was once outside. Some of what's inside will remain alien to us. For most people want the child that they never knew they wanted, or claimed they didn't want. Schopenhauer's will to life threatens to become an abstraction, where Freud's theory is genealogical and can be traced backward from an individual and its particular history. As such, Freud's theory explains why some parents do not keep or want their child. Individuals are different, and the Schopenhauerian will to life doesn't always dominate or completely determine us. Not everyone wants to live or procreate. There are multifarious forces in the world, and they can be grouped in various ways. Anti-life forces and violent forces are as prevalent as Eros. Freud's theory makes room for our rationality and our irrationalities as well as rational and irrational forces running throughout the world. Contradictions abound because there are contradictory forces, drives, desires, and interests throughout the universe.

So far, we have survived as a species and we are individuals. We understand what this means as we search for other individuals compatible with us. When we find each other, we are happy as two, but with little chance to stay merely as two. Life is bigger than we are. And it's probably a good thing as, at some point, most people will wish they had others to take care of them. We all age, and we all get weaker. No man is an island. Even so, an old man can live on an island, if he has children and grandchildren taking care of him.

This is vitally important for Freud. We are vulnerable. Freud says the need for the father's protection is the deepest need in us.[82] That's the condition required for us to exist beyond birth. A fortunate child feels like a god when it is little. As so primitive, its needs are primitive. The ability to have awareness of suffering is through primordial sensations, and as soon as the child is picked up or given a blanket or milk, it forgets that it was ever dissatisfied. Small children don't need to forgive as they can't even consciously remember, and they don't understand causality. Nonetheless, the child intuitively picks up on the fact that making certain sounds and doing certain things can prompt someone to serve it. The child finds a way to get all its needs satisfied. It has no reflection or ability not to be a simplistic narcissist.

---

[82] *Civilization and its Discontents*, p. 36.

It is pure id. Notwithstanding, the id is not idiotic. At some point the child senses , understands, and figures out that she or he is the opposite of a god. Some never consciously completely believe it, but their actions betray that they understand it only too well. Similar to the oceanic feeling, the infant is operating under an illusion. An illusion made possible because it's underde-veloped in human terms. In other words, the only reason it feels like a god is because its needs are simple and immediate. When it realizes that an outside force is needed to keep it warm, feed it, protect it, and everything else, it has a crisis. It cannot even walk or speak, open a door or use a toilet. However it can scream. When adults scream, one cannot help but see what infants they still are, with their red faces and their shrill voices. We wish we could just give them a pacifier. Adults have crises too, and many remain full of fear and resentment. An infant has a chance to evolve but it must go through stages. Humans must develop. In the case of infants, they understand in their bones that they need a protector. They learn quickly how to comport themselves to avoid pain and suffering, and they learn how to give themselves plea-surable opportunities. This is characteristic of animals. Our cats and dogs act in ways that will endear themselves to us. Infants aren't ontologically special. The go-to person for security is generally a father figure. The father's a good first candidate to model. The father is strong and seems free. Children look up to their fathers. Meanwhile the mother serves them and serves the father. They want to continue being served rather than to grow up and serve others. Still, it doesn't take long to see that dad is not unusually powerful and wise. He is not as free as he initially appeared, and not so happy either. He is mortal. He gets hurt. He suffers. And, yes, mom bosses him around too. Furthermore, he's not always nice. He causes suffering and pain. Without a deeper imagination, without a vision of life outside the family you might ask the question: why go on living? You feel powerless, and with nothing but a future like your parents isn't necessarily inspirational. Still, you recog-nize that the world is larger than your immediate world. There are other forces and agents who become candidates for admiration. It keeps building, perhaps, to the notion of Fate. Fate is quite an attractive idea. An abstract notion of fate can work wonders for some. Most people, at some point, need something more concrete in life. Monotheism makes for a strong candidate as it posits a perfect God. We are fools for perfection. God is omnipotent, omniscient, and omnipresent; that's big stuff. And Christianity throws in the trinity, making Jesus a concrete example of how to live and whom to follow. Everybody pines for a cool mentor.

According to Freud, this is the origin of religion. We invent God so that we can go on living. It is literally God as father. This idea is very intuitive to many people, and besides the existential attraction, there are the practices, rituals, communities, and stories that pull people toward the faith. It gives us a reason to be moral, a motivation to love and develop friendships, it gives us tools to temper our aggression, and it eases the anxiety concerning mortality. Freud worries, though, that it creates as many problems as it solves. It asks us to give up too much. Religion's goal is not to avoid suffering in this life, so it doesn't satiate that instinct. Religion typically also has other prohibitions that are difficult to accept. It is, from a practicality standpoint, needlessly prudish. It puts scary thoughts in one's mind. It causes stress over hell and other such punishments. There's something bizarre about someone watching you constantly. It tells us we are broken, which Freud would agree with, but the cure to our brokenness is not rational or very interesting. Religious people often end up on a roller coaster of sinning and forgiveness, of sinning and repenting. During the highs and the lows, devouts relish the rush. They feel alive. However, the wants and needs are infantile and fit too nicely with a consumer capitalist society, which promotes a type of narcissism. For the pious, all that matters is an individual's relationship to God. It denigrates this world for the next. No one else is really privy to the secret bond with the savior. It prioritizes God's law over the world's laws: I can tell myself anything and then convince myself that God will understand and forgive me. This includes murder. This logic negates civilization. It bears anti-civilizing tendencies.

In terms of love, Freud says that religious teaching runs counter to the real love of two people. It's tantamount to adding a third person. It becomes a perversion. Loving God entails loving everyone else. Extending love to neighbors and strangers becomes downright dangerous and naive. Still, Freud credits religion for taking on the human condition and trying to make sense of it all, as well as to civilize us. Still, Freud argues it requires denying human nature. He finds the phrase "Thou shalt love thy neighbor as thyself"[83] completely bewildering. He asks: Why should we do this? What good will it do us? How shall we achieve it? How is it possible? For love is "something valuable to me which I ought not to throw away without reflection. It imposes duties on me for whose fulfillment I must be ready to make sacrifices. If I love someone, he must deserve it in some way."[84] Freud, as a pragmatist, wants our relations with our neighbors to stay on point. Our relations should be based on the use another has for us, both in terms of work and sex. Loving one's neighbor as oneself doesn't get to the root of why we have relations with others. It expects us to give to others even when it's

---

[83] Ibid., p. 91.
[84] Ibid.

not rational. Freud emphasizes only caring "about others who care about us." Religions, aiming to follow God, prescribe that we "care about everyone without worrying about if they care about us." We can see the value in both perspectives. Freud and traditional religions begin from different premises. The latter defends our inherent goodness while Freud argues we are fundamentally aggressive. It's hard to decide who is closer to the truth but our survival instinct prompts us not to take unnecessary risks.

Freud contrasts his smaller circle of love with religious love. He says, in normal circumstances we should love a friend's son, as the son's death would hurt our friend and so would also be our pain.[85] Notwithstanding, Freud doesn't see the logic of loving someone we don't know or the son of someone we have never met. He's not trying to be heartless, he's asking whether it's actually possible to genuinely feel pain from the death of those we know nothing about. He's asking if it's just and appropriate to do so: if someone is a "stranger to me and if he cannot attract me by any worth of his own or any significance that he may already have acquired for my emotional life, it will be hard for me to love him. Indeed, I should be wrong to do so, for my love is valued by all my own people as a sign of my preferring them, and it is an injustice to them if I put a stranger on par with them."[86]

There are pros and cons to having neighbors. Some we know and some we do not. Some we wish we didn't know. Some we wish we did. Various things can happen when one tries to love one's neighbor as oneself. Freud is probably right to be suspicious. There's an ancient story, told in multifarious forms, called "The Lover's Gift Regained."[87] We can articulate it today as such: A married couple moves into an upscale tract home in Southern California. A single man is their neighbor. The neighbor is attracted to the young and beautiful wife. The husband, working in the entertainment industry, neglects his wife and controls the finances. One day the neighbor sees the wife alone outside in her yard. He smiles and asks her if he can be intimate with her. She says, "Sure, tomorrow, but I need $1000." The next day the man comes over and gives her $1000. He's satisfied with his day. Clearly the wife has adapted to living in Orange County. That evening her husband comes home late and asks her if the single neighbor came by earlier in the day. She thinks to herself "Oh no!" She tells the husband "Yes." The husband asks "Did he give you $1000?" Trying to hold things together, as they have a prenuptial that will leave her with nothing, she says "Yes." The husband replies, "Great! He came by my office early this morning and asked to borrow $1000.

---

[85] Ibid., 91-92.
[86] Ibid, 92.
[87] Inspiration for this comes from Chaucer's version of The Shipman's Tale.

He promised to repay before evening. We have a good neighbor. I love our neighbor."

Managing Aggression

Freud would not be surprised by this story. He clearly had a lot of people treat him badly. He's very distrustful of others. He thinks that strangers, in principle, are unworthy of our love, and that those we don't know are more likely to be hostile towards us and intuitively hate us. He says most strangers will show us no consideration. "Indeed, he need not even obtain an advantage; if he can satisfy any sort of desire by it, he thinks nothing of jeering at me, insulting me, slandering me and showing his superior power, and the more secure he feels and the more helpless I am, the more certainly I can expect him to behave like this to me."[88] Because of this premise that others will harm us if they do not know us or if we are not powerful in relation to them, he is completely against the maxim "love thine enemies." He sees it as a type of weakness or sickness. Freud, in a footnote, cites the poet Heine, who explains that he needs very little to be happy. A nice little cottage with a good bed, fresh food, and outside his window some natural beauty, perhaps a few fine trees, will make him content. And contemplating if this simple life would be enough to make him forgive his enemies from earlier days: Heine says it would. But then he adds that "if God wants to make my happiness complete, he will grant me the joy of seeing some six or seven of my enemies hanging from those trees. Before their death I shall, moved in my heart, forgive them all the wrong they did me in their lifetime. One must, it is true, forgive one's enemies—but not before they have been hanged."[89] One does not need to take one's imagination so far as Heine does to acknowledge the bizarreness of loving one's enemies. We might read it as a metaphor for letting go, for forgetting. Why would our enemies deserve our love? We understand that something psychological is going on when we have the impulse to love them. First, fear is an unconscious factor. If I love them then maybe they won't harm me. Second, we all know we have harmed others and made enemies. What if they want to hang us? Better to promote a philosophy of love of enemies to protect the self. In any case, if we stretch love to include those who want us dead, that's forcing the word "love" to do a lot of work and it's forcing the human animal to do the same.

Civilization needs morality. Without higher norms and limits, humans will regress to the lowest common denominator. We can get morality wrong

---

[88] *Civilization and its Discontents*, pp. 92-93.
[89] Ibid., p. 93.

by being too strict or too loose with it. Freud thinks that the norms of religions will be too big of a burden for many in society. Still, he understands the value of repression. Freud wants to appeal to both the devils and angels in us, but he emphasizes tempering the demons through threat of punishment. He understands the dual nature of sexual desire. Sex is a different sort of activity. It carries layers and layers of psychological, emotional, social, cultural, as well as physical weight and energy. It can pull us up to the heavens and down into hell. Our lack of understanding of the true meaning of sex, our nonchalant attitude toward anything sexual or anything involving love indicate that we have simply flipped from a Victorian morality to a consumerist amorality. There's a reason "The Lover's Gift Regained" story still speaks to us. It touches the deepest levels of intimacy and betrayals in civilization. A good society would not take sex or love lightly. It wouldn't use sex to sell automobiles or alcohol, but maybe soap. It doesn't make us prudish to say there should be limits on the exploitation of sex and love. Today's society tries to shame us if we dare even mention putting restrictions and prohibitions on what's sexually acceptable. When a Methodist politician is willing to celebrate songs like WAP, it's either an extremely cynical move to get elected or a sign of being deplorable. Words matter. Reversing words doesn't make them true or aesthetically pleasing. Responding to any human attempt to get people not to act merely on id desire by calling it inequitable "shaming" is sophistry. Unfortunately, having no shame is a virtue in our society. Asking people not to dissolve completely the public/private sphere is not intelligible to those who have no inner life. Those who think that posting is living and externalization is freedom have to show everything. We are not arguing for a Puritan morality here. Our whole life need not be obsessed with morality. Regardless Freud recognized that losing sight of the truth of our sexual nature would lead to a slippery slope of losing sight of love and morality itself. It would lead to us questioning whether anything is wrong.

Getting up each day, and not stealing, cheating, or killing anyone, shouldn't be too onerous. We dupe ourselves if we abstractly blame structures today to justify people's bad behavior. Agency exists. It should not be that hard to be decent. No structure in America today is so powerful that we can use it for justification when a person kills another. Everyone knows it's wrong to kill other people. And when we start to rationalize some cases, Freud would remind us of an episode in the French Chamber debate where, after a passionate speech to abolish capital punishment ended, a man from the gallery yelled out: "It's the murderers who should make the first move."[90] We all need to make the first move when it comes to things that are obvi-

---

[90] Ibid, p. 94.

ously problematic, otherwise we debase ourselves. But the American Capi-talist ideology of profit can make idiots of us all. We are masters of deceiving ourselves when money, ideology, and institutional power are at issue. Today there are academics who claim to be "supporting women" by arguing that sex work is just work. It shouldn't be critiqued, judged, or analyzed any differ-ently than any other labor. We can imagine someone yelling out, in response to today's trendy liberal feminist, "Let you be the first to take the job!"

Freud is clear that if we value civilization and individuals, we should encourage love and non-perverted relationships between human beings. Most people will be happiest as double individuals and most children will be better off with two mature parents. Religion gives transcendent reasons to try to move us in the proper direction. Some political ideologies attempt the same. Both religion and political philosophy understand that individuals in society need love but they also understand that we are aggressive crea-tures. Trying to support the former while dissipating the latter is not an easy task. At first blush, it seems Freud is like the anti-Jesus. Jesus spent his days talking about peace and love and didn't seem to have a job, let alone a career. He did have a vocation, though, and that was to spread the Word. Freud was more concerned with aggression, stressed working, and didn't have any expectations of peace on earth. Still, as we saw above, Freud does have a solid place for love in his theory. We might venture to say that Jesus had a strong sense that humans were aggressive, otherwise why else would he need to stress peace and love and tell us to love even our enemies?

Communist Aggression

Freud argues that the deep truth driving both religion and politics is that "men are not gentle creatures who want to be loved, and who at the most can defend themselves if they are attacked."[91] Rather, we are endowed instinctually to be aggressive. The neighbor is not only a potential helper or sexual object but also someone "who tempts them to satisfy their aggres-siveness on him, to exploit his capacity for work without compensation, to use him sexually without his consent, to seize his possessions, to humiliate him, to cause him pain, to torture and to kill him. *Homo homini lupus.*"[92] This Hobbesian intuition that man is a wolf to man is hard to refute. Armed with this idea that we come out of an aggressive and id-driven state of nature, Freud ends Chapter Five of *Civilization and its Discontents* by critiquing Communism, which he sees as making the same fundamental mistake as

---

[91] Ibid.
[92] Ibid., pp. 94-5.

religion. And although he has no sympathy for the politics of communism he has empathy for some of the ideology and gives us food for thought about all of it. He says, the problem with the communists is that they believe "man is wholly good and is well-disposed to his neighbor; but the institution of private property has corrupted his nature."[93] Freud argues that those with private wealth, of course, have power that easily corrupts them, and he admits private property will cause frictions between neighbors. Those with less, as they realize they have less, will rebel in hostility as they would against any oppressor. As such, Freud understands the argument to get rid of private property. One could reasonably conclude that if you get rid of private property you might get rid of much hostility and ill-will. Freud cautions that the problem runs deeper than private property. We will always find something to pit us against others. Pascal said: *Le moi est haïssable.* Sadly, anything can make us hateful. If it's not private property, it will be partners, it will be kids, it will be the cars we drive, the clothes we wear, the labels we make up: Take away one thing that divides us and we will find another. Freud claims this is because we are naturally aggressive and competitive, but also because we all have differing strengths and talents, both physically and mentally: "nature, by endowing individuals with extremely unequal physical attributes and mental capacities, has introduced injustices against which there is no remedy."[94] People have trouble admitting this fact and so will be *a priori* resentful despite evidence to the contrary. People tend to overestimate their own strength, skill, and intelligence. Therefore, they will feel exploited often when in reality, they are not. Further, for those talented, it's not natural to hold themselves back when they are superior. We see this in children. If a child is faster than the other children, she or he will win the race. It's dangerous to push an ideology where we ask people to limit or diminish their qualities, talents, and capabilities. It's absurd to teach people naïve versions of equality, liberty, attributes, characteristics, and structures.

Against the actual existing communists, Freud argues that it's not going to dissipate violence simply to blame social conditions. Our animal ancestors were not all pacifists and I doubt any of us want to encounter an angry chimpanzee inside or outside of proper society. We live in a very affluent society, in historical terms, and yet we have mass shootings, basically every day. In all other societies, similar violence occurs every day. There is nowhere on this planet free from violence. Nowhere. We can blame the structure of society but this is to misunderstand structures. We cannot ever erect a structure that will guarantee nonviolence. Things we think might dissipate it can turn

---

[93] Ibid., p. 96.
[94] Ibid., p. 97.

out to exacerbate it. The nature of reality is such that we cannot control everything and cannot predict much. The idea that we are not naturally aggressive and violent is a metaphysical one. We might forget this from time to time. Freud reminds us: "cruel aggressiveness waits for some provocation or puts itself at the service of some other purpose, whose goal might have been reached by milder measures. In circumstances that are favourable to it, when the mental counter-forces which ordinarily inhibit it are out of action, it also manifests itself spontaneously and reveals man as a savage beast to whom consideration towards his own kind is something alien."[95] We outmaneuver ourselves when we forget that this is not limited to any individual, group, race, or people. Everyone's history is bloody, and every family genealogy has murders and everything else sprinkled throughout the tree.

Freud's empiricist instincts remind us that we can witness this inclination to aggression in ourselves and we should therefore assume it to be present in others. It's a factor that disturbs our relations with neighbors and forces civilization to expend lots of energy to keep it at bay. If pacifistic love could be spread out like confetti at a party, without any backlash, then this probably wouldn't happen. But love too can just as easily give birth to violence. Within any relationship complications, jealousy, competition, and resentment exist. The consequence of this "primary mutual hostility of human beings" is that civilized society is perpetually threatened with disintegration. And, of course, specific societies will exacerbate it. The American fetish for guns ensures that we never put the brakes on our aggressive, competitive, and egotistic drives. Instinctual passions are stronger than reasonable interests. We love whom we love because we love them. We favor our own and think our way is superior and our people are better and smarter. This can be a sweet thing. It's charming to see parents gush over their little one as if their child were the first human to ever walk. It can also be anything but sweet.

We will never love a stranger like our own child. And one who attempts it turns into Mrs. Jellyby. The maxim "love your neighbor as yourself," in either the Communist or religious variety, is problematic on many levels. Still, we understand the impulse behind both. Civilization has to manage our aggression, and one strategy is to convince us to forget our non-relational death. If I identify with the group, almost in an oceanic oneness, not only will I be less aggressive but I might sacrifice my life for civilization. This is one of the contradictions of civilization. We must be willing to sacrifice, but not always. You and I are individuals. Civilization has an interest in making us forget that ultimately each person has an individual identity and specific life. Freud warns us against ideologies that dismiss the individual and "incite

---

[95] Ibid, p. 95.

people into identifications and aim-inhibited relationships."[96] This fetish for tribal and muddled identities has today bizarrely morphed into irrational power throughout academia, corporations, newsrooms, and government agencies, filled with busybodies, inciting people into fad and market identifications.[97] They push not so much "aim inhibited" but rather market-uninhibited seductions and restrictions. It's in other peoples' advantage to trick us into identifying with their preferred labels, with their projects and goals. Putting us in their tribe will give them power. However, will it help you seize your particular life? Or will it pull you away from your uniqueness and prevent you from engaging with things of substance? The aggressive style of the commandments from *nos petits bureaucrates* proves Freud's relevance today.

Freud offers us a trenchant critique of the contradictions of living within a civilization. Still, his theory shares foundational elements to the philosophy of Marxism. Akin to Freud, Marx's philosophical theory is rooted in human history and the problem of scarcity. Freud, and Marx alike, see that labor is central to our humanity. But while Freud focuses on the price we pay when some do not carry their fair load, and when sex and love become trivialized, Marx focuses on the price we pay when those working are not recognized for their labor, when they are exploited, and when they do not labor with freedom. A Capitalist system can only help us evolve so far. It can be a strong system for securing basic needs, but it is obsessed with profit, and so pushes us back into the id. It perpetuates selfishness, greed, and infantile desires. It doesn't help us grow into mature adults. It does not make us more virtuous.

Against Marx, a Freudian could argue that Capitalism, as consumer driven, does, in some ways help lower aggression and violence. It sublimates these tendencies into harmless competition and consumption. This works the libido and takes some of the sexual aggression away too. Capitalist societies produce all kinds of outlets for pseudo-sexual activity. A Freudian might argue that most people want to stay infantile and probably cannot outgrow that impulse. Capitalism keeps civilization pumping and sublimates what Freud sees as unalterable human instincts. This is where the philosophy of Freud and Marx come into tension. Freud doesn't trust that most people can evolve into full human beings. Most people know the true standards but choose to follow the infantile ones, and he expects this to always remain the case. Marx thinks that, at some point, given the proper social conditions, the false standards, the id pleasures, and the deep aggres-

---

[96] Ibid., p. 96.

[97] For an exquisite critique of this phenomenon, from a Frankfurt School perspective, see Alex Stern's "Critical Theory and the Newest Left," in the *Hedgehog Review*. 6/25/2021.

sion will become uninteresting to us. We will want more. We will want truth, justice, nobility, and excellence. We will want human greatness, not just material wealth. When we look at the NBA we see athletes who have material wealth. Regardless, for many of them, that's not enough. They want to be champions and they want to develop their game of basketball as a noble pursuit. We see the excellence in many NBA players and the drive for Socratic greatness. We also see the opposite.

The Communist Manifesto argues that we should be striving for a world "in which the free development of each is the condition for the free development of all."[98] The goal is not to lose our individuality but to grow it. This is only possible in a decent civilization. Individuals and society must challenge an uncivilized id and correct the irrational aspects of the superego. Concrete love is an action that helps individuals evolve, sublimate, and adhere to rational norms. Love can pull us deeper into the human condition. Through real relationships we are compelled to develop our qualities, capabilities, and a virtuosity that make us lovable. Staying lovable means continuing to evolve as a unique individual worth loving. Love connects us and reminds us of exactly why we love who we do. We see each other as irreplaceable individuals. At the same time this is not the complete story of the human condition.

Everyone must live his or her own life. In relation to others we strive to be irreplaceable. We achieve this in some relationships. Still, on another level, it's impossible. We are all expendable. If my spouse dies, I will probably remarry, or not. Either way, life will go on. Our neighbors can get on fine if someone else moves into the house next door. The team can find another point guard if a player gets hurt or traded. At the same time you cannot replace you. More importantly, everyone has to die her or his own death. Death is the only thing that is truly not relational.[99] Ultimately, it's about you: when you die you will miss yourself, so to speak. Your death is permanent for you, as you will never finish any projects or goals still outstanding. No one can accomplish your life for you. Your death is yours alone. This knowledge is in us instinctually. That itself will create a creature with some aggressiveness, will it not? This is an existential Freudian insight that reaches to the depth of your very being and mine. It is not a happy thought. Nevertheless, it is crucial that you and I come to terms with our mortality and its implications if we want to be fully human. This is a true identity.

---

[98] Marx & Engels, *The Communist Manifesto* (Bantam Classic, 2004) p. 36.
[99] Heidegger, *Being and Time* (Harper, 1962).

Chapter 6 — Seeing (Double) is Believing

> And now, I think, the meaning of the evolution of civilization is no longer obscure to us. It must present the struggle between Eros and Death, between the instinct of life and the instinct of destruction, as it works itself out in the human species. This struggle is what all life essentially consists of, and the evolution of civilization may therefore be simply described as the struggle for life of the human species.[100] — Sigmund Freud

Freud develops his thoughts on the instincts[101] around Friedrich Schiller's line that "hunger and love are what moves the world."[102] Our ego, or rational self, is directed toward self-preservation and the interests of the individual. In this way hunger keeps us in ourselves. Yet it is love, widely construed, that pushes us to reach out for objects and reproduce. Thus, while hunger captures the instinct preserving the self, it is love that preserves and perpetuates the species. Freud calls the first an "ego-instinct" and the second an "object-instinct." Both have evolved to be equally at home within us, and both, perhaps surprisingly, harbor aggressive elements along with unifying aspects. Hunger and love, besides helping us live and thrive, are part of what make us naturally aggressive and anti-life. People kill for love and for other objects, including food. We might also ignore our hunger and starve from loss of love and from loss of self. Freud is trying to understand the relationship between Eros and Thanatos, as well as how each relates to ego and object instincts.

---

[100] *Civilization and its Discontents*, p. 111.
[101] In Chapter Six of *Civilization and its Discontents*.
[102] Ibid., p. 104.

Useful Dualisms

With these goals in mind, Freud could have drawn deeper from Schiller and his "Kallias Letters."[103] In these letters, Schiller speaks about the forces of unity and destruction in terms of the beautiful and the sublime. It is through our interactions with beauty that we can come to a deep understanding of unity and harmony. Beauty, as a promise of happiness, pulls us toward the good and connects the ego with the object, perhaps using the same instinct that we saw in the oceanic feeling.[104] The sublime works in a similar way but stresses differentiation. It can capture the ego. The power of the sublime is the power of grasping one's self, in relation to what's daunting and outside us, in both pleasure and pain, but without being overwhelmed by fear. Through distance and human reason, it invokes a profound feeling of awe and joy. The sublime, as witnessed but not consumed, interacts with the immense and overpowering forces of nature (or something akin to it). It provokes a true meaning of differentiation and individualization. The experience of the sublime is as deep and meaningful as the anticipation and recognition of beauty. Both beauty and the sublime touch us in our deepest instincts, especially when understood in concert with the Freudian terms of Eros and Thanatos. The specific experiences of beauty and the sublime are the particulars of which Eros and Thanatos are the universals. Together they are as essential as they are ambiguous for *la condition humaine*.

A less poetic articulation of instinct analysis is in the simple dualism between pleasure and pain which Socrates noted in the *Phaedo*.[105] After being unchained while in prison, he rubbed his throbbing and aching legs. He observed how pain is often followed by pleasure, and how difficult it is to imagine one without the other: When you think you have life figured out, you find out that the pleasure you mistook for a simple in-itself is being held up and trailed by a pain you cannot shake. Socrates feels relief from his bondage, but he will also die that day. He is ready for it, and he insists on living until the end. He's been writing. Yes, Socrates has been writing. The guy who everyone says didn't write a thing actually did. Language and precision are important. Socrates never wrote philosophy. Nevertheless, in prison, he wrote some poetry. Through his poetry he is seizing his final moments of life, despite being trapped in prison. He is living beautifully and sublimely; he is creating something higher, without fear or resentment. Besides having

---

[103] See Schiller's, Kallias Letters (1793), at The Schiller Institute, https://archive.schillerinstitute.com/transl/trans_schil_essay.html.

[104] The question as to if it's the same instinct that can be pulled in opposite directions or two different instincts is an open question. It's worth considering Nietzsche's analysis of instincts in *Beyond Good and Evil* (Vintage, 1989).

[105] See Plato's *Phaedo* (Oxford, 2009).

art and his philosopher friends, he has his family. His wife Xanthippe is with him, as is his baby. These elements give us, thanks to Plato's writings, a vision of totality, of a noble human being who lived a full human life. He learned a craft, served his nation in war, found his calling in philosophy, had a wife and children, and spent his days searching for truth and living justly. He avoided the false standards and he lived in accordance with the true ones. He exercised *la vie philosophique*. Further, it happened because of and through each particular context, either beautiful or sublime, dancing with the gods of Eros and Thanatos.

Getting back to the poetry, though, Socrates says he is putting Aesop's fables into verse. He is expressing deeply human articulable truths to music. In prison, surrounded by death and fear, he is an individual instance of sublime beauty. The conversation turns to death and the existential question of suicide. Socrates understands how precious life is and reminds his interlocutors that one's death is about more than one's life narrowly conceived. He pitches it in terms of our responsibility to the gods. The higher things that make our lives truly human lives are what matters. Our lives need to be coherent with what is truly meaningful and real. We will all die, and life is, partly, a preparation and meditation on death. Or, as Socrates puts it, "a practice for dying and death."[106] Notice how dying and death are two different things. Dying is a process, it is part of the becoming of existence. It is also a part of the becoming into nonexistence. It is part of the change and flux we live our lives through. By contrast, death is a nothingness. It ends us. It stops all our projects. It terminates all our relationships. It is something I must do for myself and in myself. Socrates understands life's complexities. He comprehends that human life is only coherent within the structure of human mortality. Rather than pinning on the structural inequity of our fate, Socrates sees and lives free, and above the base instinct to blame all on others or on gods. Only when we grow past these immaturities can we take up a philosophical conversion and live in accordance with true standards. The prison scene introduced in Plato's text opens the door for a conversation between Socrates and his friends on fundamental dualisms that make us human: mind and body, pleasure and pain, beauty and the sublime, Eros and Thanatos.

These dualisms take historical shape in all of us. In our modern context, the world discloses them most readily as between *ennui* and shock,[107] or in contemporary jargon, boredom and outrage. We are an immature culture

---

[106] Plato, *Phaedo*. Project Gutenberg, Retrieved April, 10, 2023, from https://www.gutenberg.org/files/1658/1658-h/1658-h.htm.

[107] See Georg Lukács, *Writer and Critic* (Merlin, 1978), Preface p. 13-18.

and cannot see the higher truths except through watered down clichés. We can understand why our youth flock to horror films in a desperate attempt to feel something. To feel something, rather than to be merely stimulated, is not so easy today. Hollywood's Blockbuster movies, unfortunately, move us from the frying pan into the fire, as superhero films are deadly boring and horror films are pathetic stimulants. Together they serve up, in a predictable and tired formula, a pornographic distortion of the human condition. They are violent as we are violent. We don't believe in love so all we have left is hate. Infantile escapism or superstitious fear, while chomping on so-called snacks that taste like cardboard dipped in motor oil. Why waste your time seeing what you have already seen? Why pay money to be scared? Do we like being frightened? *Pourquoi?*

Film has become nothing but a stooge for capital and a quest for celebrity. It's a sham industry that is finally admitting that it doesn't believe in aesthetic values. Like all of us, it had to choose. It began with artistic merit, seeking to capture important aspects of the human condition and our potential to be decent humans. It had some success. Then it discovered the money that could be made. Things turned, and the philistines[108] won. Hollywood today screams: beauty is suspect. It mistakes stupid violence for the sublime. It doesn't know that the experience of the sublime is not one of being scared; it doesn't make you jump out of your seat. Rather it draws you into a proper relationship to beauty and toward a human place in the world. Today, beauty and the sublime cannot be seen on an American screen because they speak a foreign language that is untranslatable to those lacking a human language and a human ear. Hollywood is autotuned so that those in it have the exact comprehension as a chatbot. They sound somewhat coherent, but when really listened to, they are as coherent as someone commenting on how well a submarine is swimming.

The way back to dry land requires action and human engagement. That is why athletic excellence has not completely succumbed to barbarism. Athletes are not mere shadows on a screen but are living, breathing people who have trained, without reductionist university classes, so their skills in themselves transcend hollow entertainment. With sports, we see pleasure mixed with pain, but we see it in its higher truth. The entertainment industry (which includes the news media) is an animal. Schiller describes the animal as motivated solely in reaction to pleasure and pain. This can take the form of profit or loss. Human beings have reason. We have the ability to see ourselves in our world. The animal just runs from pain, runs to eliminate

---

[108] For an interesting analysis of this concept, and a partial critique of this project see Malcolm Bull, *Anti-Nietzsche* (Verso, 2019).

it. In a Cartesian alley-sprint it escapes or it attacks; it lives on a narrow yet dualistic path, alternating between boredom and shock. Humans can live in a different forest. A human world, where one can hold on to the pain of life instead of trying to deny it or escape it. Nietzsche said we can stand pain when it has a purpose, and Schiller sees the purpose as grounded in an ethical understanding that pain can be harnessed by human reason and human spirit, so that we can gallop through life. Today, rather than harnessing our pain, we rent it and share it. It's rented because in today's reality, we are incapable of feeling what true ownership means. We must, therefore, appropriate someone else's pain from the past; a hurt that we have chosen to borrow for our weak pleasure. We simply use it to roar, as we have no interior in which to keep it and no higher place in which to put it.

In the most sensitive of societies, we have lost our senses. Though not completely. The Super Bowl itself is an excellent event. Despite the brutality of the sport of football, or perhaps because of it, we experience the beautiful and the sublime. When a team puts a play together that results in a touchdown, it is a magnificent moment of human harmony. While, on the other side of the scrimmage line, the sublime is captured in the bodies and faces of the defense as they are being overwhelmed. There's nobility in the reaction, the breakdown, the desperate attempts to prevent the catastrophe that cannot be prevented on a particular play. When there is no stopping the offense's force, there can still be an elevation of the human spirit, on both sides of the scrimmage line. Even the team being overrun, despite the pain and failure, is necessary for the transcendence. We cannot always win. Not succeeding can be a sort of Socratic practice, a meditation on and preparation for death. In the game, both sides hold on to their pain, they use their reason, spirit, and experience to continue to strive forward. The team that scores gets that Socratic flip into pleasure, and how sweet it is for the aching muscles. The scoring team is never tired after crossing the end zone.[109] The team that couldn't stop it carries that pain and uses it to fight into their future. They too will have their moments of beautiful pleasure. Everything is fleeting and ephemeral in a universe like ours. Still, everyone on the field is successful just for being in the Super Bowl game. That's the truth in the cliché that there really are no losers when the game is excellent. Those who win have earned beauty and harmony, and those who lose proved their superior nature, just in getting there, as well as in refusing to succumb to mere pain. Both teams end up heroic and with human dignity in such moments.

---

[109] A better example is a 400 meters sprint race. Watch most any Olympic finals of this event and we will see the one who wins is not nearly as exhausted as everyone else in the field. This event is brutal and beautiful, as it forces one to sprint a quarter mile. Winning is the only way to have a chance to avoid the pain of it.

Stars on both sides invoke admiration and receive further opportunities. Just as pleasure needs its pain, the sport needs both teams. Meanwhile those attention starved pretenders, who don't need the money, those narcissists not playing in the game, continue to debase themselves on our flat screens as they bring advertising horror and comically-obscene gyrations into our living rooms. *They* are the true corruptors of the youth, but *they* will never be prosecuted.

The Super Bowl is an incredibly complex event that brings out the best and the worst of the human species. Of course, some events, situations, and instincts are not so ambiguous. Some are to the rim with goodness and some are patently evil. Still, there are occasions where the pleasure we feel in seeing another suffer is not simply base. The example of a football game above captures this. It doesn't make us sadists if we feel pleasure from watching a painfully powerful hit on a quarterback (especially when it was on Tom Brady[110]). Schiller says this is so because, although our reason tells us that pain and suffering are to be avoided, we also have the sensibility that understands this is not completely possible in this life. We cannot become excellent if we sidestep pain and suffering. Tantamount to a great work of art that provokes something higher in us, a good sporting event brings out something we needed bringing out. It gives us the understanding of the value of suffering, as well as the beauty of harmony and success. It teaches us about human community and individual free will. Without Eros and Thanatos none of this would happen. They work through us, as we through them. Freud is pushing our post-Christian world to see this truth. For if we lose it, we lose our *raison d'être*.

Genesis

Freudian instinct theory is contrary to the Christian notion of our inherent goodness. The Christian message is one that conceives of our creation as perfect, as made in the image of God. It's a beautiful image to contemplate. In Genesis II we are told, "And the LORD God formed man of the dust of the ground, and breathed into his nostrils the breath of life; and man became a living soul."[111] This is a poetic and beautiful vision of our coming to be. It settles in us a notion that we are meant for something higher; that we are inherently noble even as we are connected to the soil. We are not just soil, we have God's breath of Life emanating through us from

---

[110] And not just because he evokes ambiguity, but because it also shows that even the greatest is vulnerable.

[111] *The King James Bible*, Genesis 2:7., Project Gutenberg, https://www.gutenberg.org/files/10/10-h/10-h.htm#The_First_Book_of_Moses_Called_Genesis.

our first breath until our last. Then we go back to the soil and the circle is complete. As an image, and as inspiration, it's hard to beat. Nonetheless, there is a flaw or a missing piece. We live lives that are not perfect and not in the image of God. Whether God is imagined or real, we are not God, and we are not anything close to being omniscient, omnibenevolent, omnipresent, or omnipotent. What really was this breath of life?

Genesis II continues to explain, in its own way, that the breath of life contains Eros and Thanatos. Initially, it seems more simple and straightforward. We received life in a place that, at first glance, appeared perfect. We were put in a marvelous garden but quickly warned that "Of every tree of the garden thou mayest freely eat. But of the tree of the knowledge of good and evil, thou shalt not eat of it: for in the day that thou eatest thereof thou shalt surely die."[112] This complication is quite fascinating, and it's helpful in moving us into deeper waters of human meaning. It's reminding us that we are fortunate to be alive, and the earth will nourish us, but also that we need to be smart and choose carefully. For there are dangers, and the dangers grow right in the center, in the middle of everything. A tree containing knowledge of good and evil is right within our grasp, and eating from it will fundamentally change us. Further, the change won't be a positive one. We will die.

In a sense, this story of our origin is consistent with an evolutionary theory. We came from another species. At this point in the drama, we are without knowledge of good and evil, and so are not quite a human animal. A few lines later, after the creation of Eve, we find out that Adam and Eve are not ashamed of being naked in front of each other. Again, this supports the notion of a childlike or even pre-human moment, and that being fully human, as we understand it now, has essential features that at some point we didn't have, and that other creatures don't have, and that we could lose. We evolve, we have evolved. And yet none of it was written in stone. The story denies teleology or a predetermined directionality to human life. There are choices to be made. Maybe Adam, or his helpmate (as Eve is called), will eat of the tree of knowledge, and maybe not. As we are looking backward to understand who and what we are, we know what must have happened. Today we reach back for Freudian or Christian assistance to help us make sense of our lives. Both visions of human life force us to look back to try to find coherence with what we are today. They both continue to speak to us today.

Genesis spells it out directly. We did eat from the tree. We were induced by the outside, in this case, a snake that acts as Thanatos, or a will to power, trying to expand its power. The snake seduces Eve into eating the apple.

---

[112] *The King James Bible*, Genesis 2:16-2:17., Project Gutenberg, https://www.gutenberg.org/files/10/10-h/10-h.htm#The_First_Book_of_Moses_Called_Genesis.

God and the serpent each have aspects of the other. It's not an absolute binary. God is perhaps being a little unclear when he says: "for in the day that thou eatest thereof [from the tree of the knowledge of good and evil] thou shalt surely die."[113] If he means die one day, fine, but it doesn't sound as if he is saying that, it sounds more likely that we will die "that very same day." Perhaps, not a huge difference cosmically, as both entail we become mortal, but we see a vagueness here as well as an ambiguity. Further, in being told we don't have knowledge of good and evil, it is suggesting that we are not complete. Didn't we get a complete breath of life? Doesn't a human need knowledge of good and evil to be fully human? Doesn't the desire to know something run deeper than making a simple conscious choice? Isn't knowledge itself good? And even if not all knowledge is good, isn't knowledge of what's good, good?

The biblical story is both descriptively and normatively layered. It's subtly suggesting that Thanatos runs as deep as Eros in adult human beings. A human life requires unhappy knowledge and vicissitudes. Adam originally did not and could not possess complete human attributes until and unless he ate from the tree. Or could he have left the garden without eating from the tree? Would that have prompted the awakening also? Was the devil always in the garden? Aren't snakes beneficial to a garden? In any case, the story suggests that eating from the tree was a condition for becoming fully human. Then, what are we to make of the serpent? Of course, it certainly was not very nice to pressure Eve to eat from the tree. Yet we might conclude, if we need the knowledge of good and evil to really be human, that there was something good in this more seemingly Thanatos-like goading. The meaning is layered. The serpent says that God is being deceptive. Satan argues that Adam and Eve really won't die, rather: "Ye shall not surely die. For God doth know that in the day ye eat thereof, then your eyes shall be opened, and ye shall be as gods, knowing good and evil."[114] Both God and the devil are using language fallaciously or at least strategically. In the case of Satan, he's being honest that one will not die right away and that one will gain some deep knowledge, perhaps godlike knowledge. At the same time, he's also being deceptive in that it might have been nicer for him to tell Eve: "Well, eating the apple will mean you will die one day, and you won't be godlike if that means like some superhero." It's as if these two, God and Satan, took a class on "how to win an argument" and are formulating statements along the manner of the fallacy of "complex question." Similar to the lawyer asking: "Are you still beating

---

[113] Ibid.

[114] *The King James Bible*, Genesis 3:4-3:5., Project Gutenberg, https://www.gutenberg.org/files/10/10-h/10-h.htm#The_First_Book_of_Moses_Called_Genesis.

your wife?" or the sly classmate saying "Do you want to study tonight for the exam and go out for a drink?" God and the devil are packing so much into their claims that Adam and Eve never had a chance. Their heads must have been spinning trying to make sense of it all. Trying to figure out bizarre rules, the existence of forbidden trees, talking snakes, and thinking through the existential implications of it all, puts a lot of pressure on beings who don't even quite realize they are naked.

Freud pitches his theory of instincts against the Christian theory, and argues that his story is more coherent. He is right that, at least at the beginning of the narrative, the Christian story has trouble explaining the omnipresence of aggression in the world, let alone a death instinct with a capital T, as in Thanatos. Freud admits that initially he himself didn't want to admit the possibility that we were, at our base, aggressive animals: "I remember my own defensive attitude when the idea of an instinct of destruction first emerged in psychoanalytic literature, and how long it took before I became receptive to it."[115] Of course, who wants to think of themselves and those around them, and everyone in fact, as inherently aggressive and violent? The Christian interpretation of our aggression, as we saw above, is fairly coherent when one gets through the first three books of Genesis. Nonetheless Freud points out that philosophically there is still the problem of the origin of evil if God is perfect. The both famous and infamous "problem of evil" has been around for thousands of years. If God is all-knowing, all-powerful, and all-good, then how is there evil in the world? It seems God could prevent evil, would know how to prevent it, and would want to prevent it. Yet if we admit there is evil, then logically something has to give.

True, we could deny that there is evil in the world. That seems to deny empirical reality. Or we could put limits on God's power, goodness, or knowledge. Doing any of these takes away some of what we traditionally want from God or believe God is. Freud's solution, if we can imagine him within a supernatural schema, is to defend a sort of Manichean view. There must be two equally powerful Gods in the universe, and they are battling it out. What Freud will not do is deny that our aggression exists and, in fact, he insists that the aggression goes all the way down. It's a version of the ancient story explaining what holds up the world.[116] The answer to what holds up the world is that the globe rests on the trunk of an elephant. The follow up question of what holds up the elephant is met with the answer that the elephant balances on the back of a tortoise. Of course, the next question is: what holds up the tortoise? The answer is that it's turtles all the way down!

---

[115] *Civilization and its Discontents*, p. 108.
[116] Georg Lukács, *History and Class Consciousness* (MIT Press, 1971), p. 110.

That's what Freud thinks about aggression. We are aggressive through our roots and the world is inherently a dangerous and violent place. Fortunately, Freud also finds in humans that Eros runs just as deep. This implies we will never solve the war between Eros and Thanatos. We will win some, and we will lose some battles, but the war is eternal. We have to find a way to live, while keeping as much aggression at bay as possible. This prompts him to reject any radical or utopian solutions. He also concludes that we will never act consistently good and that we are destined to keep dreaming of a better world than there can actually be. Happiness then will never be absolutely obtainable. Christianity says something similar about our time on this planet, but tries to mediate the pain of it by offering heaven as hope. At the same time, it hurls the threat of hell to temper worldly aggression. If Freud is correct, this can work for some, but it will also create certain fears and neuroses that will make it hard to experience deep human beauty or face the truth of death.

Myth and Reason

As we saw above, ancient stories and ideas still help us make sense of our lives. And Freud still helps philosophers conceptualize the human condition. Freud has been incredibly influential in philosophy, and he is a pillar in the critical theory of the Frankfurt School. We will briefly look at the Freudian influence in Horkheimer and Adorno's masterpiece, *Dialectic of Enlightenment*. Besides drawing on the best of the philosophical tradition and Freud, it also incorporates the Homeric tradition. As such, it taps into our noble past and allows us to ponder another dualiam: myth and reason. The ancient Greeks, as pre-Christian, had an alternative vision of human meaning. Horkheimer and Adorno utilize Freudian categories to develop their social critique of modernity and to analyze the human quest for happiness. They also follow Freud in utilizing a layered hermeneutic approach to articulate our need to make sense of our lives. As does Freud, they trace a story of humanity that runs along parallel lines to that of the evolution of an individual. They argue that we first came to understand the world mythically, and our vision of happiness came out of id desire sublimated through supernatural beliefs. Western philosophy and science didn't develop until the 4th century BCE, but stories have been around, so it seems, forever.

A mythic way of understanding the world and ourselves is deep and intuitive. It is grounded in a sense of humans as part of a larger story. The key to the story lies beyond the human realm. The universe is too complicated for humans to understand on their own. Reason, too, is limited in a magical world. We need inspiration and guidance from poets, chosen ones, and higher beings. We need to look to nature as a model and to respect it as a superior force. The appropriate relationship of humans to gods and to nature is for us to mimic, worship, revere, and assimilate.[117] We must know our place in a world that is greater than us, and we must not challenge the hierarchy or disrupt the balance of the universe. We must understand our subservient nature and accept that we are but pawns in the eternal struggle between Eros and Thanatos. If we are good and lucky, we will side with the sacred, and when we lose our way, we may get overtaken by the profane. As in the biblical story of Genesis, knowledge is not simply a positive power, but knowledge is also a potential trap leading to our downfall. Knowledge leads to hubris. By not seeking rational enlightenment we are enlightened, and in not treating knowledge as power, we are knowing.

While deference seems to be a style rooted in modesty and nobility, as it stresses a decentering of humans, a sense of unity, and reverence with and between outside forces, it's more complicated than that. Horkheimer and Adorno point out that admitting and succumbing to greater powers in the world is a strategy to survive. It's not necessarily based on reverence and humility. Under the guise of a sacred positioning is the quest for self-preservation. One accepts the mythic picture of reality because one has to. Like a child who obeys out of fear, we accept our fate, until we realize we don't have to. Horkheimer and Adorno say, "Mythology itself set in motion the endless process of enlightenment."[118] Our spiritual relationship with nature, the world, and others is, at least partly, strategic. We think it will help us survive, will allow us to be successful during the hunt, or will ensure it rains on the crops, and so on.[119] Similarly, the oceanic feeling, the sense of unity, oneness, and lack of alienation, screams vulnerability as much as anything. It exposes the human condition more than it reveals a transcendent metaphysical reality.

Consciously strategic or not, a mythic approach to reality sometimes works pretty well. Even today, positioning oneself into spiritual institutions and interpreting events through a mythic schema is common and socially smart. The mythic allows us to connect with something greater, it protects the ego, and it pushes back existential grief. It plays well with the instincts of most others, it gives us places to go and conversations to have, and it serves the purposes of securing existential meaning, while often encouraging moral behavior and acceptance of our fate. Mythic thinking is everywhere

---

[117] Horkheimer and Adorno, *Dialectic of Enlightenment* (Stanford, 2002), see esp. Ch. 1 The Concept of Enlightenment, pp. 1-34.

[118] Ibid., p. 7.

[119] Ibid., pp. 5-11.

today: Trinkets, incense, spiritual beads, crystals...are everywhere. These bagatelles allow people to view the world through a tantalizing, totalizing schema or simply take a short trip to a magical land, to escape from our mundane modern world. Astrology is as popular as ever.[120] This may seem innocuous, as it "brings" people together as with all identities. People are searching for connections. Yet instead of cleaning up the mess of our lives, we "invent" groups. These fabrications give others an unqualified authority over us. People will think they know me simply because of what "star I was born under." They will say, "Oh, you are a Capricorn, that means you are..." Whether it is true or not, this belief has power so long as people feel it is true. It's a loophole, though, an avoidance behavior not to create deep links with others. It is easier to invent identities and pretend play through such shallow relationships. Mystic generalizations don't forge true friendships and relationships.

We have never given up on the mythic, and we probably cannot, as we all begin our lives as id creatures. At some point though, in our collective history, we tried another way. Rather than seeing the world as having essentially greater powers than humans, we began to see ourselves as powerful beings in the world. We questioned the gods and the supernatural realm. Rather than worshiping the world, we began to see the world as an object for our desires, wants, and needs. We developed, what Horkheimer and Adorno call a "strategic" or "instrumental" relationship to nature. We disenchanted the world.[121] With our new power we could challenge the gods and try to outwit them. We could question the rules of nature and cheat a little. We invented new rules as we changed our perspective from one of reverence toward the world to one of utilizing it as a tool for human needs and wants. This allowed us more power in our actions. We used human reason to structure what seemed chaotic. The world became a canvas for us to paint our values and human meaning onto. This gives birth to science, and to philosophy, as schema to live by and through. The world, as demystified, looks very different from a mythic world. It allows for new practices and institutions. Of course, by demystifying the world we lost some of the magic and mystery of existence, but we gained power in survival, in understanding nature, and in satisfying pleasure. The 18th century Enlightenment proper saw that each scientific discovery was good, in the same way that Genesis 1 exclaims after each piece of creation: "And God saw that it was good." Enlightenment rationality became the new God, the answer to the riddle of life, and the new

---

[120] One might argue that today's DNA testing and ancestry matches are Astrology for the "educated."

[121] *Dialectic of Enlightenment*, Chapter One: The Concept of Enlightenment.

meaning of human existence. We became the explicit masters, the rulers of the universe both in production and ideology. We are the descriptive and normative standard for existence itself. The sacred gives way to the profane. As Marx and Engels detail in *The Communist Manifesto*, "all that is solid melts into air, all that is holy is profaned, and man is at last compelled to face with sober senses his real condition of life and his relations with his kind."[122] This signals a new age, and yet it also hints that things are more complicated than the Enlightenment promised. Linear progress was a lie. Sobriety means we abstain. We avoid certain pleasures. At what cost?

Modernity conceived of itself as a power, it declared knowledge was a power.[123] We constructed ourselves and the world with stronger armor, while perhaps weakening what was under the armor. Modernity is progress and decline. Not only do individuals start out without reason, but our civilization is in many ways still medieval. Paul Ricoeur points out that Marx was a master of suspicion[124] who didn't trust that the momentum of enlightenment thinking would free us. Yes, capitalism is the necessary path to a better world. Still, Marx saw that it couldn't end with capitalism, and that the journey would be an unpleasant one for many. We won't evolve unscathed. Still, Capitalism in all its destruction is a necessary evil. We are creatures who need to get a handle on our world, we need to defeat scarcity, and only then can we be free. Marx is not naive about how difficult the process will be, but he knows there is strength in numbers and people fight back when all is taken from them. He saw that things would come to a head in industry. Freud, as another one of the masters of suspicion, understood the inside of the human as well as Marx understood the outside. Horkheimer and Adorno draw from both to give a complete picture of the problem of modernity and to give us a road map beyond it, even though they themselves doubted we could read it.

Horkheimer and Adorno see the mixed blessing of modernity for what it was and what it became. Survival becomes an end in itself. Staying sober counts as a win. As an end in itself, living becomes an instrument to simply keep living. However, we don't live forever. Without a higher purpose, we lose the ability to derive substantive meaning from our lives. Sobriety is not a higher purpose. It's a condition for a higher purpose. But the Enlightenment forgot to keep the higher purpose when it poured out all the alcohol. As puritans, we pushed forward and muddled through. Even so, how long could this last? Our id and the mythic were waiting in the wings; they were

---

[122] Marx & Engels, *The Communist Manifesto* (Bantam Classic, 2004), p. 17.
[123] See *Dialectic of Enlightenment*, p. 1-2.
[124] Paul Ricoeur, *The Conflict of Interpretations* (Northwestern University, 2007).

hiding under the covers of our prudent and reasonable world. Eventually, we saw our future as a choice to remain steadfast or return to id pleasure. Most have chosen the latter. Those who have chosen the latter still have strategic rationality in them. The individual remains central, holds dear to its cunning and scientific self, and mixes back into myth and superstition. The Copernicus revolution, combined with a return of supernaturalism, creates an astrological logic of each individual as Sun God. Just as myth always contains elements of cunning reason, rationality has always retained superstition. Enlightenment treats science, math, and secularism with God-like reverence. It blocks out anything that doesn't fit this schema, just as much as the old world view did. If both schemas share such bias, can we speak of truth? Can we live in the world and see that world for what it is in itself? Do true qualities of people, things, and the world matter? Are they even intelligible? Can we speak of progress?

Today true qualities and capabilities don't matter. We supernaturalize strategically according to our abstract ideas, and id-driven desires. As mythic-strategic, we have nature, others, and even ourselves as a canvas to post on. Someone is always in the center of the pic during a selfie. This manner of Being creates individuals who are cunning, mythical, narcissistic, and laced with sadomasochistic tendencies. Horkheimer and Adorno see the twentieth century as the culmination of this type of individual, but they trace the beginnings of our "evolution" all the way back to Homer. They contrast the *Iliad* with the *Odyssey*. The *Iliad* captures a different sort of individual. As the hero of the *Iliad*, Achilles is a warrior. He lives according to his attributes and sense of justice, for which he is willing to die. He does die for these principles. The gods give him the option of avoiding his fate at Troy in favor of living a long and quiet life as a farmer. Fighting in the Trojan War would have made him a hero, but it would have also ensured that he wouldn't survive past the war. Similar to the choice in Genesis, it's a real choice. Achilles knows himself. Thus he chooses based on his qualities, capabilities, his sense of virtuosity, and his loyalty to his people. In the *Odyssey* we are told, when Odysseus visits him in Hades, that Achilles regrets his choice. Maybe. Maybe Odysseus is lying. Odysseus, as wily and cunning, is a master at telling fibs. He uses language to his own advantage. He treats the truth in the same manner that he treats his crew. He ushers in new and vastly different values for human beings. He makes these new values attractive and dominant.

Horkheimer and Adorno detail these new values through Odysseus's encounter with the Sirens.[125] The Sirens represent the mythic, the oceanic,

---

[125] See *Dialectic of Enlightenment*, pp. 25-27.

and the other side. A traditional encounter with Sirens would end in death. The Sirens bring Eros and Thanatos together in one fully lived moment. It captures the beauty and sublime nature of existence. It promises full and complete happiness until we can no longer resist the haunting music and bodies of the Sirens, until we get devoured by them, or smashed into the rocks to dissolve into and with the ocean. As with Achilles, the traditional approach is warrior-like in its focus. Everyone knows their place and no one debases him or herself in the name of survival. No one survives. Therefore, the question becomes: am I fulfilling my duty while alive? Everyone goes down fighting as an individual self. Odysseus rewrites the script. He is "enlightened." He wants to be the author of his own life. He wants to speak his truth. He debases himself. He takes on a false identity. He lies, he is cunning, and he thinks he has a right to do anything and be anyone. Context and duty don't matter. I want it, I'll do it. In his performance to the Sirens, he tricks them. Similar to someone with floor seats at the Lakers game, without any knowledge of the game, Odysseus tied himself to the mast of the ship so he could be there and then post about it later. In this way, he alienates himself from the deeper poetic world. The only story he can tell about it is an abstract one: "It was great, man! I was there!" We get no details. Meanwhile Odysseus's crew is exploited as they do all the labor so he can have his celebrity moment. The workers hear nothing with their ears full of wax. They labor without beauty or happiness. We have always used gods and others to get what we want; the most interesting Freudian aspect of the story is how Odysseus outwits himself. He has a moment, while bonded, in which he realizes that he is sacrificing too much.[126] You cannot be happy tied to a mast. You are not fully an agent when impotent. You cannot experience beauty or the sublime unless certain conditions are met. Taking shortcuts is just a sign of immaturity. As Horkheimer and Adorno put it: "The overripeness of society lives on the immaturity of the ruled."[127] Odysseus didn't allow himself to participate fully in that moment as a vulnerable agent. He did not act ethically, and he traded in living for celebrity. In this way, he turned himself into a mere thing. At the same time, his larger journey, like ours, was one of vicissitudes. Can we train ourselves to simply not be gluttonous and impatient? Can we train ourselves to wait until the moment is ripe? Can we get it right before we are overripe and rotten? We might understand our existence in terms of a fruit

---

[126] However, he hadn't prepared himself for a higher moment. Odysseus let himself be driven by his carnal id for too long. Whether with Circe, Calypso, or even Penelope, Odysseus let his sexual impulses dictate his life. With the Sirens, he wanted them without being devoured, so he settled for their song. Thus, he was seduced without being touched. One could trace a pathetic line from Odysseus to modern strip clubs to virtual sex today.

[127] *Dialectic of Enlightenment*, p. 28.

on a tree, knowing to pick it at the right time. Otherwise, life will be insipid. As for any good harvest, time, work, and patience are essential to experience your life in its sublimity.

Homeric tales give us deeper insight into the true nature of a noble individual. I must see what orchard I am part of, what type of tree I am, what fruit I can bear, what the soil below and weather above are offering to me. There are trees of every sort, and in the correct environment every tree can be upstanding, exalted, and sublime. Nobility is not a class value. Anyone from any class can be noble. Nobility is in fulfilling your highest function. Your focus cannot be on mere survival. You cannot just use other people. You must let agents be agents. You must treat objects as the objects they are. Simply trying to survive, using others, manipulating things for exchange value, pursuing celebrity, wealth, and social success reveal a tree that is diseased. Being useful, pursuing excellence, and using your qualities and capabilities in coherent and higher ways is nobility. It is not noble to push my base id desires into and onto the world. Making situations about myself, forcing everyone else to adjust to my belief system is undignified and dishonorable. Rather we need understanding of the world, others, and ourselves to be noble. As captain of the ship, Odysseus had a duty to his crew and he needed to have an understanding of the mission he was charged with. When people embark into situations with arrogance or hubris, things go wrong. Odysseus lost every single member of his crew before getting back to Ithaca. Everyone else died from his motto of "I'll do me and you do you." At the same time, he lost his individuality. Sadly, he lost it the minute he was trying to seize it. He conceived of himself as an independent and rational agent unto himself, and yet he failed. He roared his name out to the Cyclops to claim his individuality, yet his name was distorted. He called himself a "nobody" because, despite his self-interpretation, at that moment he was nobody. He was nobody because he was neglecting his responsibility as captain. Instead, he was pressing to get recognition on the big screen. He couldn't just leave quietly with his men. He had to make a scene. Numerous humans suffered from his one-man show. Individuality and nobility only develop from out of higher contexts where I fulfill my role. Emphasizing ornamental things doesn't make an activity higher or better. It distracts from the good of the situation, and risks corrupting the event itself and spoiling the human meaning, as one's life sinks deep into the ocean below.

Getting home, surviving, but losing his crew, made Odysseus a different and lower Greek than his predecessors. He became bourgeois.[128] He survived every individual hurdle, which boosted his personal statistics. He returned

---

[128] See Ibid., Excursus I: Myth and Enlightenment.

home with material riches, but also poor as his team was literally lost at sea. The Homeric story of Odysseus is so powerful because it shows us both the successes and failures of the human condition. If Odysseus failed with the Sirens and with his crew, he succeeded with Penelope, his father, and his son. Akin to Odysseus, we will not live perfect lives. Nonetheless, if we occupy virtuous places, and focus on nobility and maturity, we can evolve and return home relatively unscathed. Sometimes, though, it makes you greater if you have the strength not to leave home. Staying and caring for those who matter to you is a higher quest. Some know to stay home, and know how to dwell with those people and things that are real, and that they have a history with. Things and people that you understand, that are suited for your capabilities and qualities, and that connect with your traditions, make for an ocean of meaning, without ever having to get on a boat and head out into a storm. This may not sound exciting, as the culture industry loads youth's minds with infantile fantasies. Today's "priests," those insisting on steering the boats of our lives, occupy the deck, live on the surface, but never bother to open the hatch to see what's below. What if we take the tiller of our ships from them? What if we take the helm ourselves? Surely they will starve. Superficiality is conducive to celebrity and the latest trends. Meeting new people, going new places, I can always sell myself as interesting, myste-rious, and deep, without really having to be interesting, mysterious, or deep. Around strangers, nobody can pretend to be somebody.

Perception

The cunning manner of perceiving the world, initiated by Odysseus, has deeper roots than social and mythic history. Perception itself has cunning built into it. We are organisms that take advantage of our ability to see. Human survival might depend on it. Human perception, though, is not immediate.[129] In other words, we are not blank slates directly capturing all of reality. First, perception only captures a piece of the world at each moment. We see what's in front of us. It takes the imagination, memory, and more, to make sense of what we are literally seeing. We see the front of objects and our minds fill in the details. In this way, we might think we're seeing more than we are literally seeing. I might tell myself: I see Mireille at the *boulangerie*. Strictly speaking though, my eyes capture the front of a human form that reminds me of my friend Mireille. Organisms naturally see what they need to see in order to survive and get along in their world. They don't naturally see

---

[129] This section is inspired by *Dialectic of Enlightenment*, Elements of Anti-Semitism: Limits of Enlightenment.

much of what is irrelevant to their lives. There is always more going on in any environment than what we are paying attention to. Just as there was more going on in the past than we are often willing to see. Further, to see well we need to be awake and not distracted. Our eyes physically must be strong and healthy. In some environments we can see better than in others. It's hard to see underwater or in crowds. It's hard to see with a weak, distracted, and cluttered mind. What we think impacts what we see. What we see impacts how we think, what we think about, and if we can think at all. We bring our own experiences, wishes, hopes, and so on, into perception. Our emotions, memories, and the unconscious impact how we perceive. When I say "I see Mireille," there's probably emotions attached to it. Maybe we had an argument the day before. This may prompt me to "see" her as dressed badly. I may think: "Really, who wears a Lakers jersey to a bakery?"

When walking in a packed basketball stadium, trying to find my seat at the game, my senses are alert and I'm reacting to others trying to find their seats. It develops a kind of quickness and positioning, especially if the seats are not assigned. We might compete for a good spot to view the game. I may be thinking: will the people sitting around me be friends or foes? What team will they be rooting for? It's not a great time or place to engage in philosophical reflection. This is the place for what Heidegger called "idle talk."[130] Idle talk captures the phrases and conversations we employ when going about our day. It's the meaningless banter we exchange with each other. Heidegger says it's the language of the "they." The "they," or the *das man*, captures our ability to speak and act in the manner that *one* does in our society. In other words, it's the ability to engage in mindless chatter in civilization. There's nothing wrong with this in moderation. Idle talk allows us to pass on, perhaps in our own way, things everyone already knows or believes: "Anthony Davis needs a big game tonight if the Lakers are to beat the Denver Nuggets." The discourse of the "they" is necessary to blend and interact with each other, and it's only a problem if that's all we do.

We cannot constantly have conversations that matter. We need to be able to share the little, obvious things so that we all see each other as common humans. In the same way, we need to warm up the body before playing basketball. Anyone can pull a muscle if he or she doesn't warm up. However, if all we do is small talk, or all we do is warm up, we are wasting our time and our lives. You cannot be either too serious or too playful: moderation and balance are needed. *Un peu de détente après une journée de travail, non?* The *das man* will try to pull us into their world of fixating on what's popular and caring about what's superficial. As long as everyone is doing it

---

[130] See Heidegger, *Being and Time*, (Harper, 1962) [V. Being-in as such, 35. Idle talk].

or talking about it, no one has to feel guilty about it. Much of what passes for important discourse in society (especially through the media and entertainment industries) is meaningless, a distraction, and financially a waste of resources. Idle talk repeats the same clichés in the same way the culture industry repeats the same shows and entertainments. They just update them to fit with the style and fads of the day; they'll do anything to keep us gazing at them. Some mistake this for progress and respect. Still, most of us realize how shallow it really is, as we strive to do things that are more serious and worthwhile. Whether Anthony Davis plays in the game or not has no true bearing on our lives. Regardless, many fall completely into the mode of the *das man* and live lives trying to keep up with it all. When this happens, the *das man* has won the game of cunning. And those who got conned will never see for themselves or live as autonomous selves. I cannot become an individual if I get obsessed with being part of the "they." To live authentically and freely you and I need to push back on the banalities tempting us. People can forge themselves into individuals if they have true strength. Deep, honest, perception and the right environments help us move beyond the platitudes and into true understanding. When I am at Joshua Tree National Forest and I look up at the sky, I realize how far I can see. I can literally see for miles and miles. If it's a calm and quiet night I can think slowly and clearly. If I am surrounded by just a couple of other people I know well and can trust, we might look each other in the eyes and speak truthfully and deeply. All our senses can come alive. We are not manipulated by stimulants nor are we being bombarded with roaring simulations. There's no need for mindless or polite chatter. Discourse that's authentic can reveal new ways of being. It allows us to think about our futures. We can consider different courses of action for our lives. We can go deeper into the imagination and use our eyes to take in beauty just for the pleasure of it. We have more control over our perceptions and we can begin to see beyond them.

The idea that perception always involves selecting and filling in the missing pieces is not necessarily problematic. Maybe I'm at the game as a true fan, and so I'm really focused on watching the game. I block out everything else and zone in on my favorite player. I can gain a profound understanding of how he moves and what makes him great. Or, maybe I'm only there because I want to talk to the person next to me. I might not see the court even though it's almost directly in front of me. The game affords us the opportunity to catch up and reconnect. Asking what we are looking at and why we are looking at it helps us avoid falling into the traps society sets for us.[131] When we use our free will to focus on things that are good for us, when we take responsibility for our projections, when we enhance our individual qualities and develop our talents, when we understand our needs, interests, and duties, when we ask questions of relevance, coherence, and truth, when we are able to think against ourselves and against the world, when we are capable to think with ourselves and with the world, we are practicing philosophy. This art of living philosophically not only elevates our everyday lives, it also influences the world beautifully. Only then can we clearly see the promise of happiness.

---

[131] Horkheimer and Adorno draw directly from Freud's theory of instincts to describe what they call "false projection." See *The Dialectic of Enlightenment*, Elements of Anti-Semitism: Limits of Enlightenment, for an extraordinary account and analysis of "false projection."

Chapter 7 — From Animals to Humans (and back?)

> Why do our relatives, the animals, not exhibit any such cultural struggle? We do not know. Very probably some of them—the bees, the ants, the termites—strove for thousands of years before they arrived at the State institutions, the distribution of functions and the restrictions on the individual, for which we admire them today.[132] — Sigmund Freud

When we compare ourselves to other animals, we don't really envy their lives. Of course, from time to time, when we have to get up and go to work or school, we might look at our cats and envy a life that doesn't have to deal with colleagues, clients, taxes, grocery shopping, traffic, and all the rest of it. Nonetheless we understand that a human life is something that we cannot seriously trade for an animal life. And yet it's difficult to live the depth humans are capable of. Religions try to pull us out of our animal state; some have posited reincarnation but we know, after reading this much about Freud, we can't uncritically accept this. We also have the philosophical trend, that claims it is following Heidegger, and posits an object-centered philosophy. This too runs the risk of falling into a performative contradiction. In the very act of claiming to center my analysis from another object or species I must, by definition, use my own subjectivity to motivate it. It's clear, subjectivity is always already connected to the world, but the framing is a human one, and each person is materially autonomous; we never completely get outside the ego, our body, or the species. Further, there's no getting to Being-in-itself.[133]

---

[132] *Civilization and its Discontents*, p. 113.
[133] Heidegger may have also proved there's no coherent writing about it, either.

Anthropomorphic Language

No worries. Living through a human perspective isn't so bad. We have to carve up the world to live in it; we have the ability to achieve this well, which means striving for and accentuating our highest humanity. We are always interpreting reality, and there is always more than one way of looking at things and accomplishing things. What if we see what's important and do what's best? What impact will exercising this consistently and regularly have on us as individuals and on our communities? What will the world become? What will we become? We can evolve, become something greater, and create with beauty and depth. We can make existence better. What exists, exists. Then, there are certain things we can bring into existence. For example, when Picasso started painting in a manner we call Cubism.[134] The materiality of the world didn't change for him to do that. There was always the possibility to carve up reality that way, if the right creature, with the right tools, came along to make it. Of course, it took natural talent, intelligence, care, dedicated work, history, others, and some luck. Still, Cubism is a style that had the potential to be created. Fortunately for us, it exists now. Whereas, some things will never get created because they defy what is possible in the world, or the type of creatures necessary to create whatever it is never evolve to be able to realize this. Sometimes certain creatures could invent something, but they prefer not to. They don't want to put in the time, the effort, and they don't see the point. Basketball didn't have to exist in the universe. If the unfolding of the world had played out differently, basketball might not be here. If Picasso hadn't existed, painting would be different. If we have a nuclear war, perhaps there will be no paintings anymore, and there will not be a Super Bowl champion next year. Or, if humanity evolves in another direction, a higher one, no one will want to live for fame anymore. Notice that, in all these cases, you need human subjectivity and human language to discuss any of this. We have to be anthropomorphic. There's no point in running from it. The parts of the world we helped create needed us to be as they are, and the parts of the existing world we didn't create needed us (so to speak), to be defined as we define them. In other words, if we had never existed, the stars, galaxies, black holes, and such, would exist exactly as they are now. The mountains and forests still would exist if we didn't, but not exactly as today. For both groups, though, being labeled as stars, galaxies, black holes, mountains and forests is our doing. By contrast, the very existence of certain things rely or depend on us. The game of basketball only exists because of us.

---

[134] For a somewhat related use of Picasso, see Alexander Nehamas, *Life as Literature* (Harvard, 2002), p. 59.

Still, we can approach the world in different manners, even if all of it is anthropocentric. If we look at the early Heidegger we might see an emphasis on creating and living as an assertive self in the process of becoming the author of your own life, *comme Sartre*. While with the later Heidegger we could locate an emphasis on stepping back and watching, listening, and learning from the world. Even when we take a passive stance, we are still experiencing everything through our human subjectivity, but our relation-ship to the world might be altered. Through all the perspectives, we never lose the agent or the human form. As humans we are constantly taking different stances in and on our existence. Sometimes we do it consciously and sometimes not. Still, the recognition of varying perspectives gives us power. But power for power's sake doesn't equate to virtue. Taking a stance on important matters without historical understanding, and without the goal of developing and getting things right, is dangerous and reveals human immaturity. If we adopt a standpoint without intelligence, or if we fetishize standpoint, we might end up merely queering our perspective. Conversely, when we know and understand our duty toward our role, and the meaning of the context, then our subjectivities could take on a great form. Conse-quently, what's important will be granted its true value. One might argue that knowing we are interpreting will make it harder to maximize our proj-ects and goals. In this case, we might keep second guessing ourselves and looking for alternative interpretations or different ways of living. We may never become stable or deep. Reflection can halt action. Those who do not reflect or question often have an advantage.

Aggressiveness, assurance, and obstinacy often defeat talent, uncertainty, and intelligence. Yet earlier we argued that living *la vie philosophique* requires reflection, slowness, and knowledge of the true nature of ourselves and our relation to the world. How do we resolve this contradiction? We must be able to bracket what will distract us when it will distract us from the truth. We must focus and fly through the air like an arrow shot by Achilles when we have the higher bulls eye in our sights. We must be able to draw out what needs to be drawn out, at the appropriate times. If living is an art, we must practice it as an art form. We must live with beauty and create from where we are at. We must put ourselves into virtuous environments and make our culture noble. If we don't come from virtuous spaces that give us habits and forge us with strength, we will not be useful in the new and good areas we are trying to adapt to. We might have to work and attune ourselves before we can participate fruitfully. It is easier to get on the right path if we are given proper habits when young; thus it helps when one's parents and local community are reliable guides.

We might, from time to time, need to think of our lives as a totality.[135] We might need to reflect, question, and think about how our lives as a whole fit together. At other times, we will need to stay within the specific context or situation we find ourselves in. Further, sometimes we will need to question the appropriateness of the context or situation itself. We can ask questions about when and where to pursue each important thing in our lives. We can ask questions about trying to live fairly consistently. Human lives are not stories and we shouldn't try to weave a life with that sort of coherence. We are not fiction. We are living, material beings. Human life is too complex and rich to be reducible to tales or even to words. We cannot and should not try to make everything subject to linguistic articulation or deductive validity. Still, there are elements of narrative that will help us live well. Rich traditions, too, help us make sense of most contexts and give us tools to reflect on the nature of a full human life. Not being aware of where we are, where we came from, or what it means to live a human life causes chaos. We must understand the meaning of the contexts we are in to get things right, to have knowledge, and to act well. Children, from time to time, can be in their own world, so to speak, and so will act in ways inappropriate to a given situation. If children randomly scream and color in the hymn books during the church service, we have to teach them how to act properly in church. If someone kicks the basketball instead of shooting, the ref will blow the whistle. Still, sometimes acting inappropriately is appropriate. It's up to us to figure it out. There's no external or absolute standard to defer to. There are internal standards and proven traditions that can be rationally and reflectively utilized to help us. The philosophical life stresses the power of rationality. It also helps when we talk to each other with the goal of understanding and of trying to figure things out, of trying to evolve according to what we have been referring to as "true standards." Tradition embeds many of the true standards. Still it's not sufficient. We have to be critical and we have to dialogue to get things right. This is especially true in a modern and diverse world. This requires some ceding power and others embracing it. Going into a situation and trying to control it by talking every second is very different from listening to and learning from each other. Depending on what goal you have, and what the situation requires in order for it to be that situation, either could be appropriate. But most likely, when you can't stop talking, you also cannot really see what is going on. It's a sign that you are not comfortable in the environment or that you are acting narcissistically.

---

[135] See Raymond Geuss, *Who Needs a World View?* (Harvard, 2020), for a deep analysis and partial critique of this.

There are many ways to approach a situation as a human, but one way we cannot approach it is as a bat. Like bats, we have evolved from the tree of life and so we share some features. Still, our perspective and driving features are now human ones that we cannot shake off. Further, we are all individual subjects and cannot shed our individual histories, either. When we ignore this and try to lump our experiences into human groups not relevant to deeper human circumstances, we typically get as much wrong as we do right. Rather than capturing the profound meaning of our shared experiences, we start to blend it with whatever label we are attempting to identify with. Society is always pushing skin-deep sameness trends, hoping we will buy into their seasonal fashion garb. There's really no reason to think that two Americans with Irish ancestry share anything more in common than any other two people. It's not a deeply interesting reason to bond with another person. Of course, there are identities that have shared histories, but it's often exaggerated today. Growing up in Northern Michigan poor people and some others, such as guys with long hair or certain other "features," often got a talk from a relative concerning why people like them couldn't and shouldn't trust the police. We all heard stories of guys who got beaten, thrown into jail, robbed, and even sexually assaulted by peace officers. Moving down state I realized that many black males had the same sort of experience with some of the men in blue. Some experiences connect us in ways not everyone understands, if they live on the surface. As interpretive creatures, we can, of course, create or imagine contexts where any identity matters. Often, it's others highlighting the connections so they can reduce and control us. Or it's potential members themselves. Those who are not truly individuals, and those who can't find their way in certain contexts, will search for a group to create meaning or they will try to alter the meaning of the context. That's how social identities quickly become essentialist ideologies. This distortion makes us forget that identities and labels are contingent and situational,[136] and it will drive us batty.

Humans really do not want an animal life, although we can be seduced into craving elements of one. Even a seemingly higher sentient animal's existence is one of limits we do not share. Most animals cannot experience the higher goods that we can. They mostly seem to merely eat to survive, seek shelter without aesthetic considerations, and have little control over their sexual drives. Still, some animals clearly have feelings, emotions, and act in ways that connect to virtuous human traits. And our pets are amazing. The deep care, and dare I say, love that we can have for them and them for us, shows us that our roots are deeply intertwined. We are all part of the tree of

---

[136] See Georgia Warnke, *After Identity* (Cambridge, 2008).

life and there is no ontological dualism, no essentialist material or nonmaterial difference, between us and other animals. Life and the world itself exist along a continuum with many branches and intersections. Depending on my interests and projects, I can prioritize different branches. Certainly, other animals can do things stemming from their natures much better than we can, and we can do things thanks to our nature that they will never be able to do. We can be proud of our individual and species qualities and not fetishize attributes not available to us. We might want to try to develop our living human qualities rather than reduce ourselves, or mindlessly mimic other animals, traditions, or earlier ages. Capitalism tries to deny us our development. It tries to make us animal-like and it tries to keep us infantile.

Capitalism wants to control the narrative of human existence and to do so it uses one of our greatest attributes: language. It tries to get us to think in clichés and it uses products to mediate our conversations and relationships. As language becomes impoverished, so does humanity. Animals don't have language in the way we do. Human language is the only language we know of that makes truth claims.[137] The very idea of a true standard is predicated on the notion that human subjects have this unique attribute. A cat doesn't get asked, or ask herself, to justify her life. My cat doesn't have to answer when I ask why she is sitting on the kitchen counter. She can't answer. She doesn't think in human terms. She might let out a meow, though. I can interpret and attribute answers to her, but I'm projecting. This gets us back to our necessary anthropomorphism and our unescapable individual subjectivity. Unlike speaking to our pets, when talking to other people I can ask them why they are doing something, and they are expected to answer, especially if it impacts me. I might ask you a question and you might say: "None of your business." You might be right. Or, I might be able to explain why it is my business. Dialogue is a human activity. I can dig in the litterbox like my cat, but saying I should or should not dig in it puts us in a human realm. Unlike just acting in the world, people have discussions about which actions will work and which actions are appropriate. Will it really work if I dig here? Is it appropriate for me to dig here? We introduce these aspects into reality. They are vital for us to be fully human and to be moral creatures. We use words to describe the world, and we discuss the validity of the descriptions. We utilize language to talk about what we should do and should not do. Both descriptive and normative discourse is uniquely human, as moral discourse is, too.

---

[137] See Jürgen Habermas, *The Theory of Communicative Action*, (Beacon, 1981).

A Freudian "Garden of Eden"

Humans start out more as animals than as humans. We don't have language, morality, guilt, or civilization at the "beginning." To explain our transition, Freud has his own Garden of Eden story, his own "Genesis" story, we might say. The origin of guilt, original sin, justice, and the birth of civilization are present in Freud's tale. It's an upside down version of the Genesis account. It's really an anti-garden of Eden narrative. It begins like the Genesis myth, with everyone under the tutelage of a father, but in Freud's story he's a horrible one. The pre-civilization father was a brutal and aggressive tyrant who controlled the family through violence. The family existed to serve his needs and wants. The father's instincts were satisfied at the expense of everyone else's. It was an unmoral place and a pre-civilized environment. Whereas in the Biblical scenario, Adam and Eve were not anxious until they ate from the tree, in Freud's myth, we are anxious before the transformation to civilization. In fact, Freud claims that anxiety originally develops from fear of external authority. Without the origin story it is counterintuitive to claim that anxiety "is indeed the cause of instinctual renunciation to begin with, but that later the relationship is reversed."[138] In other words, we are originally anxious because we fear the tyrant father. We fear what will become of us if we lose his love and protection. This anxiety prompts us to deny our own id instincts in favor of satisfying the father's desires. Is it correct to say the tyrant father loves his sons? Isn't love patient, kind, and understanding? Isn't the tyrant father all id? He's all passion and adrenaline. How many people today mistake passion and adrenaline for love? In any case, whether or not the father truly loves, the sons do love their father. Sometimes we love what we fear. Sometimes we stay close to what we fear, as we recognize there are greater dangers further out. In the case of the sons, it's love emanating from tribalism, security, and direct fear of the father. The fear of loss of love carries with it fear of loss of life. The "original" father is a wicked will to life power that will cause a deep imprint for humanity. Still, it is what makes us develop a conscience. Since the father prevents his sons from unleashing their own violent and sexual instincts, they learn to control them. On the other hand, they pay a mental and physical price for this. To deal with it psychologically, they identify with the father. Boys especially can live vicariously through the father: "Yes, I cannot unleash certain instincts, but my father can. I'm like my father, and one day, I may be my father." Ironically, through living under the tutelage of someone violent and without much empathy, some of the sons develop a conscience. To what extent, today, do we control our instincts

---

[138] *Civilization and its Discontents*, p. 121.

simply because of fear? To what degree do we control our instincts simply because we can imagine a future where we won't have to? At what level do we control our instincts simply because we can imagine a future in which we will get revenge?

Freud's genesis story is not the most auspicious foundation for an ethical creature to emerge out of. Whether the story is literally true or even figuratively plausible, we do know that today a human conscience is a mix of instincts fighting each other. Reiterating Freud, the claim is that anxiety over having a tyrant father gave us the strength to control our instincts. This, in turn, gave us a respite of peace and inner calm. Nonetheless, denying my instincts only provides for a momentary relief. The instincts don't just die out. Rather, restraining myself eventually will become a cause of anxiety. Consider hunger; it doesn't like to be unsatiated for too long. If you don't eat, you will eventually pay a price. At first, hunger pains us, and then as we get used to fasting it can take on a pleasurable feeling. People who fast lose their anxiety and guilt as they develop through the art of deprivation. Ultimately though, you have to eat. It won't always and forever feel good to suppress desires: it will make you anxious. We are conflicted. On the one hand, we want to ignore the conscience, and on the other, we don't want to ignore the conscience. Having a conscience is a power too. It gives you control and helps build a human self. As such, the conscience makes the self feel guilty for not upholding duties to the self. Conscience too is a part of the self that wants to overthrow the father. This will build anxiety and fear. Fear of the father, and guilt over contemplating his demise can exist at the same time as my fear and guilt for not standing up for myself. Anxiety was once the cause of instinctual control, but now suppressing instincts causes anxiety. The self has evolved to control itself, it now has a conscience, but it is not free, and it is conflicted.

The parallel to Eve eating of the apple in Freud's story comes when the band of brothers overthrow and kill the father. As he explains it in *Totem and Taboo*, "A violent and jealous father...keeps all of the females for himself, and drives away his sons as they grow up...One day the brothers who have been driven out came together, killed and devoured their father and so made an end of the patriarchal horde."[139] The brothers gained their freedom through unleashing their violent instincts. It wasn't an instinct for knowledge but for something else. The sons were more body than soul. It's a dangerous moment as letting go of carnal repression can discharge wildness and madness. Unlike the Biblical story (until we get to Cain and Abel), this origin story

---

[139] Freud, *Totem and Taboo*, Project Gutenberg, Retrieved May 15, 2023. https://www.gutenberg.org/files/41214/41214-h/41214-h.htm.

is brutally violent. Where Eve gains understanding through discourse with a serpent and with Adam, and the two of them have the voice of God, the band of brothers, so it seems, don't do much talking (I'm sure they didn't discuss consuming dad). It's more likely they collectively and unconsciously tapped into their instinct for freedom and seized it without needing a tribal council. Such is the joint power of the id and ego when sexual need is denied. It isn't required to put this in a syllogism for males to understand. Adam and Eve advance in consciousness by eating from the tree of knowledge; the band of brothers do the same through a violent act, but an act that is partly done through an impulse for justice. The brothers feel and live the injustice of the patriarchal order. They come to realize their strength and power as a collective. They are stronger as a group than their father. They are able to overthrow the father, but they will have to live with the guilt. They feared and loved their father.

This is why Freud claims the conscience or superego[140] itself is aggressive. The father is the initial superego. He's an external one; he is the law of the land. He makes the sons anxious, which they internalize. It creates sons with an internal superego. This superego works, from the inside, to protect the father from the sons, and them from him. The internal superego must be aggressive, like the father, to prevent the brothers from overthrowing the father. The superego is initially a substitute father, so the internal voice carries the aggressiveness of the father in it. Still, the practical ego dealing directly with the id desires of each son will eventually push back on an irrational superego. As the sons become semi-conscious of the contradictions, they will realize that each of them has the right and need to be free. The aggressive superego can now be utilized in the service of the sons and their manhood, rather than in the name of the father. Justice toward the self and one's siblings becomes a new social norm. They don't want to simply reproduce a brute patriarchy. They don't want a world ruled by id instinct. Even so, the foundation of civilization is id instinct. Still, this superego, teaming up with a practical ego, cannot let the irrational id push things too far. The brothers kill the father, but they will not simply replace him with their selfish id. They must, at some level, understand they are the qualified authorities. Qualified authorities cannot abuse their power. Rather, it is here that one grasps a rational identity. This identity understands that it has duties to the self and certain others. At some point we must all be our own qualified authorities to seize our individual lives. Still, to defeat the

---

[140] Freud doesn't distinguish "conscience" from "superego" until Chapter Eight. The former he calls "a function" and the latter "an agency". See p. 134. Consider Nietzsche's example of "lightning strikes" to see why such a distinction is problematic.

stronger father, it takes a collective effort. Together, the group is qualified to seize freedom, and part of this freedom is in limiting aggressiveness. Self control is a power, and having a conscience becomes like controlling what and when to eat. Sometimes I need to deprive myself of food and at other times I must eat. There's a strength and positive feeling in deprivation and in satisfying needs rationally. Control means not doing too much or too little. Control itself has a violent element: "that in the beginning conscience arises through the suppression of an aggressive impulse, and that it is subsequently reinforced by fresh suppressions of the same kind."[141] Learning the difference between rational and irrational aggression is an art, and an imperfect one. One will have successful and unsuccessful days. Watching Draymond Green on a basketball court, we see that irrational aggression is always ready to make an appearance. Also, we see that Green has won four championships with his brothers.

Our interpretation of a Freudian Genesis story suggests that guilt cannot be completely eliminated. We now have consciousness and a conscience, and we cannot live without acts of violence. Hence, guilt is part of the human condition. We will feel guilt if we do nothing. We will feel guilty for obeying our father. We will feel guilty for killing the father. We will feel guilty for even contemplating killing the father. When one has options, guilt and second guessing oneself are natural. Just knowing there are other choices sends the human mind into bizarre places and spaces. Guilty feelings versus "guilty" actions get confused in the mind. In human history, it's only later on that the human mind learned to differentiate between feeling guilty for something and having remorse for something. And, we still confuse them today. Remorse is a feeling for having literally done something wrong, while guilt may exist just for thinking something forbidden. The band of brothers loved their father, they had love in their heart and, at the same time, had duty in their minds. They needed to overthrow the tyrant father because his authority was not rational or just. They helped free the group, themselves and their sisters, and they shared power afterwards. Ending the father's rule made all of them guilty and remorseful, and at the same time it gave them a sense of justice and pride. After the overthrow of the father, primal instinct doesn't go away or take over. Humans are left with all the contradictory instincts and ideas floating in and through us. We muddle through. Some instincts we must continue to renounce, some we must free, and others we must strictly control for the individual and the society to be healthy.

Thus begins the quest to be a higher human being and to have a good community. The act of violence, the origin of civilization, is unethical from

---

[141] *Civilization and its Discontents*, p. 121.

one perspective. Murder is wrong. However from another perspective, it is a first act of justice and a necessary condition to have a human world. Further, just as the religious story has its interpretation of redemption to complete the journey that began with the garden of Eden, we can give the Freudian story completion too. However, we don't have to wait for Jesus's return to vindicate our "original sin." For civilization to redeem the promise in the killing of the tyrant father, it must evolve in a higher manner in our actual civilization. Only justice, truth, and sublimated human instincts relieve and, perhaps, justify the violent origin. What if we don't evolve? If we stay infantile and base, there is no redemption and no justification for the original deed. Christians can still go to hell after Christ's sacrifice; we can still fall into barbarism. We can create our own living hell. If we are no better than the tyrant father. If we are not noble, then we too are not civilized, and we too cannot justify our actions or our authority. If sex and violence rule us, then our lives are meaningless, and we have proved ourselves unworthy as human beings. If our projects and identities are superficial or dominating, then we just are the tyrannical father. We must build a moral and meaningful civilization to absolve, legitimate, and justify the human condition.

Moral Discourse

The realm of morality is a human realm. It's a realm that requires certain types of subjects with an ability to look at the world, reflect, and act in certain higher ways. It requires beings that can describe their world, think about what that world could be, and reflect on how they want to act within it. It requires the ability to see beyond self interest. Even though there are many theories of morality, under them all lives the idea of human reason and human discourse. Without language, both descriptive and normative, we don't have morality. With language, we have internal discussions of what is right and wrong as well as discussions with others. We give reasons to each other for what we believe is moral and what we think is immoral. Internally, our moral instincts need linguistic articulation and reflection. You can dialogue, a bit, with yourself. Dialoguing with others is often more fruitful. In situations near to us, it can be difficult to be objective. Others often help us see more clearly. Knowing whom to talk to is an art. Mindless confirmation or confused and manipulated answers from others harm moral thinking. In any case, morality comes directly from us. Without us there is no morality in the world any more than there is basketball. We might think we are getting our views from God, Nature, Duty, Utility, or even think that there is no morality. Freud understood these rationalizations are partly attempts to escape our human condition. Regardless of what we believe about "moral theories," we will either be moral or not. Knowing that someone is a Kantian, a Utilitarian, a Christian, an Atheist, a relativist, an Objectivist, a Nihilist, etc., tells us very little concretely about how he or she will act in most situations. Any person adhering to one of the above theories might give someone a hard time for having long hair. Even when we think we are guided by higher principles, God, or Nature, we might not live by them consistently. Living fairly consistently is something we either do or do not do. Ultimately, as individuals and as collectives, we will either seize our moral selves, or not. No other creatures and nothing else will do it for us. Finally, what is deemed moral or not will be the result of our upbringing, social norms, nature, habits, discourse, and instincts, as well as our ability to convince ourselves and others.

Language is important. Language can pull us out of a strategic realm and into a moral one. If I tell someone I will do something, it creates a different bond than when other animals communicate. I can't make any such promises or build any such bonds in dialogue with my cat, and she cannot make any to me. Between people, it's different. I can make promises to you and you can hold me accountable for my promises. Living with others and making explicit commitments to each other changes our relationships. When we make promises and keep them, we grow virtuously and we make our environments better. When we don't keep our promises, we make ourselves and the world worse. After assurances are made, the expectations change. A broken promise or an unfulfilled commitment is more of a betrayal than when there is no commitment or promise at stake. The expectations are higher when humans enter into contracts and explicit commitments with each other. Ignoring this is to flee from the human condition. Sneaky people and deceptive people cannot be noble and have no true understanding of guilt. In Chapter Seven of *Civilization and its Discontents*, Freud focuses on the power of guilt, and on the way in which language and the way we speak to each other and ourselves makes guilt an important issue for the human condition. My cat doesn't feel guilt. You feel guilt. I do too. It's the human conscience and consciousness that gets the blame or the praise for it. Our subjectivity, with the ability to imagine other ways of being and other opportunities, creates a human world of guilt, resentment, and new forms of conflict. Our ability to break promises and contracts makes our species unique. Freud asks why we didn't develop the way ants, bees, termites or other organisms did. These creatures have types of communities and interactions without the sense of guilt, conflict, and resentment that we see in our civilizations. These other creatures cannot make explicit promises or write up contracts that they all sign. These other beings lack the linguistic attributes and individuality that we have in our societies. We are not the only organisms that live in communities. Nevertheless we seem to have bigger problems living together than many other social organisms. If we didn't have such robust language and if we didn't have such strong individualistic tendencies, human civilization might be radically different. Our attributes create a unique paradox for us. As thinking beings, we are a threat to a stable civilization. "I think, therefore I don't really like civilization" might be our unspoken motto. To counter this, a superego, a voice of power, was invented to help keep us in line. The superego acts as its own linguistic[142] and authoritative power to keep aggression under control and to prevent the downfall of human civilization. Still, it seems to come at a steep price.

Freud knows we cannot give up civilization, so the question becomes one of managing within civilization, of getting rid of some of the aggression within individuals and still allowing for individuality. How can civilization use language and our individuality to its advantage, and how can individuals use civilization to their advantage? Can both civilization and the individual thrive at the same time? Or does one have to be defeated or at least severely constrained? The starting point for Freud is that we have to recognize that aggression is deep in us. As babies we are aggressive. If we need or want something, we have no problem acting out in order to try to get it. Toddlers will bite or hit others to get the coveted toy. Eventually, we learn to use words to get what we want, although some seem to get away with throwing fits. Civilization has been clever enough, most of the time, to prevent us from releasing all our aggression onto the world. Still Freud thinks the aggression doesn't just go away. Civilization had to redirect some of the outward aggression right back into us. In other words, aggression can be used to lash out at the world, and it can be turned toward the self. *Les humains ne sont-ils pas créatifs?* Freud calls the superego the part of us that punishes the self for our aggression. The superego, in the form of having a conscience, makes us feel guilty for our aggressiveness, and it tries to convince us that we need to be punished for it. This weakens and disarms our desire for aggression from the inside. He says the superego is comparable to "a garrison in a conquered city"[143] that watches over the parts of us itching for trouble.

Freud admits that it is difficult to give an account of the origin of guilt, and his story of the tyrant father is meant to guide us. We say a person feels guilt or "sinful" when she or he does something he or she knows to be "bad."[144]

---

[142] See Jacques Lacan, *Écrits* (Éditions du Seuil, 1966) and *Autres écrits* (Éditions du Seuil, 2001). His views on language and the unconscious are worth considering.
[143] *Civilization and its Discontents*, p. 114.
[144] Ibid., p. 115.

It's more complicated, though. Some will feel guilty just from recognizing in the self an intention to do something bad. We can ask why the intention is regarded as equal to the deed. This is a Christian idea and a Kantian one. Children are told that God knows what's in their heart and this creates an idea that one's thoughts *are* deeds. If I think bad thoughts, then it's as bad as doing a bad deed. God knows either way. We even had a president who chastised himself for "lusting in his heart," while we had another one who, allegedly, slept with a porn actress and felt no guilt. *Les humains sont drôles.* There is something wise in acknowledging that we must look inward when considering the morality of a situation. We can't just look at what results from actions. We can't consider merely *what* we do. Morality seems also to be about *why* we do things. Kant understood this clearly. He stressed that we have to be careful about simply judging others from the consequences that stem from their actions. We do things all the time that turn out in ways we didn't intend. It's the nature of reality that we cannot control or even know all the effects of the choices we make. Judging other people's moral nature in terms of whether they are producing more pleasure than pain, or more goodness than badness, does not get to the heart of moral actions. Kant also recognized that if I do something for glory, or any strongly egoistic motive, it's not the same as if I have the intention simply to do good. We see, then, there is ample reason to consider motives or "what's in one's heart."

Kant takes this intuition and forces us to think about what it means to consider morality as inwardly driven. Of course, when it comes to many practical tasks or leisure activities (what Kant called "hypothetical imperatives") I can, and should, do things according to my individual desires. If I feel like eating ice cream, I can ask myself questions about how many calories I've already eaten that day. I can ask questions about my health and aesthetic goals. What I eat is a personal decision and is driven by what I want for myself. Morality is different. Unlike hypothetical imperatives, Kant argued that moral actions need to be guided by something universal and something deeper than an individual's personal desires. Moral actions, he said, need to adhere to a "categorical imperative." A categorical imperative is an action that is binding in all circumstances and not dependent on an individual's personal desires or individual goals. An example of a categorical imperative is: do not murder. According to Kant, this maxim should hold under all circumstances and for anyone. It cannot be merely grounded in personal desire or particular circumstance. Still, one can ask the question as to what exactly "grounds" the maxim. A religious person might ground it in God's law or in love for and from God. Kant prefers to ground it in duty and rationality. One might say Kant's grounding is based on a prudent God within each of us. A rational internal voice of conscience (a type of inner God) we should bow to. In this way, Kantian morality is consistent with various religious moralities, it's just articulated philosophically. The motive here, for Kant, is desiring to be a rational agent or wanting to be a higher driven person. For the Christian, being "higher driven" is to obey God. For the Kantian, to be higher driven is to follow what's rational rather than what's merely self-interest or individual desire. One formulation of his categorical imperative tells us to: act in such a manner that one could universalize it.[145] I ask myself: what if everyone did this? Would things work out in a rational way if it was universalized? If so, then my motive is reasonable and moral, and my action will be appropriate. By asking "what if everyone did this," I'm testing and validating my action through a categorical imperative. If no one murders anyone else, civilization will not be threatened.

Both religious and Kantian versions of duty and conscience can be helpful to individuals trying to ground individual moral intuitions. Both suggest that guilt is a result of not following a higher law. A law that we recognize we ought to follow guides us. Feeling guilt is understood as a way to prompt better behavior in us. Moral theories that stress looking inward can help us control our instincts. They acknowledge that thoughts and ideas are different from actions, yet they consider the former vitally important. Thoughts arise in us in spite of ourselves; we don't always choose what to think or feel. At the same time, we can gain some control over how we think and feel and what we believe. We are responsible, at some level, for all of this. Whatever arises in us can be cultivated, limited, and sometimes snuffed out. We need a vision of who we are and what we want to be like, if it is going to have any coherence to it. Staying away from certain things will help keep certain ideas and beliefs out of your mind. Tantamount to avoiding putting alcohol in your body, avoiding moral poisons gives you a chance at health. When the liver does not need to spend time and energy breaking down alcohol, it can focus on "higher" functions. When the mind does not have to try to erase a pornographic image, it can go deeper into contemplating beauty. We all know about the extremes of the internet. Avoiding things that are obviously toxic is obviously good. Avoiding toxins, including toxic individuals, if you want health, is part of living by a true standard. Using your rationality and choosing wisely what to put in your head is part of the art of living.

Still, both Kantian and religious interpretations of guilt and moral responsibility suffer from being forms of idealism. They over-prioritize ideas and beliefs. They locate morality in a nebulous realm. It's ultimately in your

---

[145] See Kant, *Groundwork of the Metaphysics of Morals*, (Cambridge, 2012), *Critique of Practical Reason* (Cambridge, 2015).

mind. Regardless, ideas, as ideas, should not be a powerful will to power. We don't make the world through our thoughts and beliefs. We make the world through our actions in the world. That's why the most important thing is what we do. If I am feeling bad, I need to move my body: work out, do something useful, get off the internet, turn off the cell phone, go help someone, stretch, practice yoga or martial arts, eat well, etc. We talk constantly about mental health, but mental health should be part of a regime of living well, acting well, and connecting to virtuous activities. We can't start with mere "mental health" if we want to fix ourselves, if we actually want health. When it concerns morality, our practices need to be central. Ethical practices, traditions, and daily rituals ground true morality. We should not be faced with ethical dilemmas every day. There's something bizarre and off about constantly questioning the motives of oneself and others. A good society wouldn't need to overtax itself with ethical banter. A society full of individuals feeling anxious, guilty, and constantly needing to signal virtue is a society of individuals with highly irrational superegos. As this trend grows and becomes nebulous, it produces a diseased, cultural superego that "stands" above us and controls us like a God watching and judging from behind the clouds. It signals the end of sunny days.

Still, it's important to analyze and understand why people feel guilty, not just for their actions but for their thoughts. In fact, some people will feel worse for their base thoughts than their base actions. Virtual reality exacerbates this phenomenon as it's an environment of quasi-thoughts and pseudo-actions. It's an in-between space and creates, as Eric Schwitzgebel labeled for other purposes, an "in-between belief."[146] In other words, something that is hard to define as either a belief or a non-belief. It's no man's land. It can be innocuous, but sometimes it turns sinister in the way stylish nihilism can spin. It allows things to percolate without responsibility, focus, direction, or depth. Living too long in a space and environment in which you can get away with not really believing and not really disbelieving things you are interacting with is unhealthy. Life functions with depth and directionality only when people put their chips on the table, we might say. Jumping from one thing to another merely creates seasonal consumers playing with surface products. The virtual world is an extension and intensification of our larger world. We can open and close pages quickly. By quickly jumping to another page, we may think we are fooling those who glance at our computer screens when they walk by. In reality, it may be the surfing self who is fooled. Mindless browsing still goes into my mind, but in an in-between way that

---

[146] See, Eric Schwitzgebel, "In-between believing," (2001) Philosophical Quarterly 51: 76–82.

weakens my individuality and freedom. It is suited to push us away from the good, as it is a realm well-suited for play-actions and inane beliefs.

Freud's analysis of morality takes on another level of philosophical sophistication when he points out that all this moral talk about motives and feeling guilty for our aggression or potential aggression assumes that we already know what is bad. The idea here is that we only feel guilty if we think we are doing something wrong, but we can ask: where did we acquire our belief that we are doing something wrong? According to Freud, we don't have an original or natural capacity to distinguish the good from the bad concerning ethical behavior. What is considered right and what is considered wrong is not written in stone (unless, perhaps, you follow The Ten Commandments). All we have, initially, for judging what is bad or good is the ability to feel pain and experience pleasure. However, pleasure and pain don't equate to rightness and wrongness. Morality doesn't work too well if I can tell myself that anything that feels good to me is good, and anything that feels bad to me is bad. For what is morally considered wrong is not always "injurious or dangerous to the ego; on the contrary, it may be something which is desirable and enjoyable to the ego."[147] We see here that there is an extraneous influence at work, and it's this that decides what we call good or bad, and right or wrong. It's not the person's own feelings, rather it's an outside influence directing what one feels into a judgment of: right or wrong. As we saw with the tyrant father myth, the motive for accepting the outside authority is that the individual feels helpless and is dependent on the outside power or pressure. It's best understood, Freud says, "as fear of loss of love."[148] If one loses the love of another person, upon whom one is dependent, he or she also ceases to be protected from a variety of dangers. The protector is by definition stronger and can punish as well as protect. In this way, the other is superior and might prove it, if challenged. This means that, at the beginning, what we later label "ethical" is simply what allows one to experience love. What we later label "unethical" is really just whatever causes one to be threatened with loss of love. For fear of that loss one must avoid doing things that will make one unlovable in the eyes of the protector. This too is the reason why it makes little difference whether one has already done the bad thing or only intends to do it. The danger and punishment only set in if and when the authority discovers it and cares about it. In either case, whether it's about thoughts or actions, the authority might react in the same manner. In this way, doing and thinking what the authority approves of is good, and

---

[147] *Civilization and its Discontents*, p. 115.
[148] Ibid.

doing or even thinking what the authority disapproves of is bad and hence wrong. Is any of this moral?

According to Freud, we are motivated to act good not because we know the good, want the good, or need the good. Rather, we are motivated from an outside source whom we want to love us. Or better stated, we are motivated out of a fear of losing the love of the other or of others with power and authority. In this occurrence, loss of love is not merely a mental or psychological loss. There are material consequences. More than a feeling, it's one's life. The child or person under another's tutelage can go hungry, get hurt, abused, or die. It's further complicated as actions alone don't tell us if one is loved. For instance, if you don't love me but act lovingly towards me, I might not be able to recognize that you don't love me. I survive for a spell and believe I have a protector. This is dangerous, though, because if the authority is not a true protector, one day he or she may hurt those of us the protector claims to care about, and those unprotected will not see it coming. Even if the authority never directly harms those being "protected," if the authority secretly doesn't care about those being manipulated, those being manipulated will probably sense a gap between the other's feelings and actions, and the lack of unity and consistency will stir up aggression. Thanatos-like effects can be directed at self and the external world. We can't always choose our "protectors." However, when we can, we should choose carefully.

Regardless of our initial protectors, we all must evolve to have a chance at a moral and meaningful life. All of us begin our lives being driven by motives that are not ethical. Our original motives for being good have nothing to do with having a pure heart or deep sense of moral responsibility. Our heart is selfish and our reason is strategic. We are not motivated by a higher spiritual intuition or a higher sense of wanting to be good. We are merely motivated by fear of loss of love. Reasoning from this premise, if the authorities taught us that being good was the exact opposite of what they are telling us now, we might very well accept it completely. If someone tells us it's right to turn the other cheek and someone else is taught it's ethical to exchange an eye for an eye, both formulas will be fully accepted as moral under the conditions in which one is trying to secure love. The Platonic puzzle of how something can be good and bad at the same time creeps back in. The lesson here is that we need to be really careful when trying to define, criticize, or justify anything or anyone simply on original motives alone. It's hard to even really know what people's motives are and what their motives were in the past. It's easy to take things out of historical context and critique them. Still, none of this implies that we should give up enquiring about motives or judging the worth of things partly from and by the motives behind the act. Purity, like perfection, needs to be uncongealed by heating these terms up with human life. At the same time, relativism or nihilism is not the answer. This is as problematic, which is to say incorrect, as idealism. This brings us back to the point that morality is a human construct that requires dialogue. No unmediated grounding, as well as no initial motive, is sufficient in itself. When we fetishize motives or origins, we end up succumbing to false standards of value. The foundation of our moral reasoning is not moral. Nevertheless we often expect the foundations of our societies to be moral. And if they are not, and they never are, then we feel we have a right to be resentful or cancel the whole deal. This immaturity exposes a lack of strength to evolve. Imagine someone breaking off a long, deep, and meaningful friendship with you because she found out that the very first time you spoke to her was simply because you found her attractive.

Social Anxiety

It's easy to over emphasize or under emphasize the significance of origins. It's also easy to mislabel them. Freud is right not to want to define it as "bad conscience" or even "guilt" when what is driving someone is a fear of loss of love.[149] It's better to understand that it is a social anxiety rather than an internal moral sense of right and wrong. This is clearly how it works in children and it seems to continue in many adults. Our contemporary panopticon world encourages such social anxiety, and it encourages us to mislabel it. We can ask if, rather than trying to come to terms with living moral lives, many today are simply trying to be "loved" by the various social communities, political communities, and virtual communities. Many communities today are tyrant fathers. Despite that, they label themselves as virtuous, and they often emphasize the maxim "self-love." These communities talk about loving each other and it's not uncommon to hear people within them, who are not truly close, expressing love for each other. They often call complete strangers "my friend." It's a good strategy for a server to angle for a better tip in a restaurant, but also it reveals an Odyssean cunning. Society tells us it's an important social value to be told that we are loved and to tell others that they are loved. Yet isn't that the secret ideology of the tyrant father? Love, directed at social relationships, is confused and ideological. It's rather meaningless. It's easy to say one loves everyone. It's harder to like everyone. The latter requires getting to know other people and living with and around them in concrete and deep ways. The same is true of self-love. Loving oneself is easy, superficial, and rather meaningless. It's more difficult to like your-

---

149 Ibid., pp. 115-117.

self. Liking yourself entails work. Working on yourself is the only way to get to know yourself and to like yourself. This project is often confused with self-confidence. Many with self-confidence do not know themselves or like themselves. Even so, they project an image and attitude in the world. Striving to appear confident in public will distract from the higher quest and make it difficult to live outside the public gaze.

Unless we become greater, moral, and mature, we will never like ourselves. We might feel anxious and depressed. Social anxiety and depression have become identities and badges of honor. Freud would remind us that social anxiety and depression might actually signal that one has no true sense of morality and no strong notion of individuality. We don't like it when others treat us as lesser or unethically or immaturely. The same holds for the self. To face myself honestly means that I must grow, that I must seek higher things. Rather than trying to overcome my anxiety through "radical self-love," I should start acting morally and putting higher things into my mind and body. Influencers, the internet communities, positivity ideology or drugs (whether prescribed or recreational) will not afford me these higher goods. Our society teaches us to run from ourselves and toward the superficial. Learning to like yourself, and being worthy of being liked, is a practice, not an identity. An identity-driven society creates intangible communities in which their members beg to be recognized, which in return give birth to thousands of people who are anxious and depressed from the fear of losing the "love" of these strangers. This type of "loving" is an abstract one, a rather easy one, because it doesn't involve the work it requires to get to know the other person as a human being. Rather, we see each other as identities, labels, logos. Freud sees these communities as tribes of sadomasochists.

In such a world people don't leave their tribe out of an existential need to flee a lower space for a higher one. They stay because they don't want to give up infantile delights. Rather than evolve, they find a group that shares their puerilities. One might think this is good, as it is nice to feel accepted. However, at the expense of the higher standards, it ruins one's life. Sadly, our world is filling up meaningless identities based on abstract recognition or on hate of others. Our society rewards this, as it fits our materialist schema. It allows "me to do me," while at the same time "sticking it to the libs" or roaring, "okay, boomer." It gives me a sense of aliveness, a sense that I belong. In reality, this feeling is merely id passion and adrenaline. In the meantime, I don't develop my individual freedom or my true morality unless the conscience grows into a wise superego.

A wise superego can unite with a rational ego and sublimate the id to form ourselves as fully human. We don't transcend in the sense that we can leap out of our skin or become essentially something alien, but we can evolve. Evolving into a full human being is one of the greatest gifts we can give ourselves. It's clear that we should not be spending our one and only exis-tence roaring, cheating, trying to win, just kneeling, indulging in infantile pleasures or seeking eternal youth. Aging and growing old are two separate things. To age is the work of nature whereas to grow old is to mature. It's the work of the individual. Going to France as a teenager and climbing the Eiffel Tower, shopping along the Champs-Elysées, and playing alongside the Seine can be wonderful and elevating at that age. But if you love France, and you should, there are deeper and more beautiful experiences that you can encounter there as you age, and this truth holds for almost any place. If you learn the language, get to know the people, their history, and you keep going back, if you allow yourself to listen, learn, and interact with that particular place that draws you into higher meaning, something magical happens: You become greater, the world becomes deeper and more meaningful, and then *la vie est belle!*

Of course, life is not only beautiful. There are complications and dangers. How the individual grows will impact society, but what society values will more greatly impact the individual. In a society that does not value good things, it will be hard to be good. If you build your inner citadel and a strong and rational superego to aid your ego, it might cause issues if those around you do not. When you evolve into someone higher, you don't need the recog-nition of all others. Still, not getting sufficient recognition can hurt your career and life. Those who stay immature and are driven by abstract recog-nition, or by fear of an external authority, may gain social perks. They also will not be inhibited by a conscience if they have weak ones (or none at all). Some adults evolve just enough not to spill their guts and tell on themselves. We see children tell on themselves all the time. It's charming. Nonetheless, those without a true conscience may develop not to tell on themselves while also not developing an inner moral compass. They become dangerous, as they have the immorality of a child without the fear of an authority figure. Mean-while, those who develop a human conscience will punish themselves. Those with a conscience inside of themselves have no place to hide. The superego can punish the self as quickly for thinking something as for doing something. It's godlike in its all knowingness. As Freud puts it, "nothing can be hidden from the superego, not even thoughts."[150] Overall, this is good. Keeping oneself moral is the road to being fully human. However, again, it puts you at a disadvantage compared to those without a conscience, and sometimes you might "over punish" yourself for just thinking certain things.

---

[150] Ibid., p. 117.

One might think that the superego has no motive to hurt the ego, as it's bound up with it. Even so, just as friends don't always treat each other well, neither do different aspects of oneself. First, even though we evolve, we don't change, in so far as we don't lose all lower aspects of even what we have improved within ourselves. The id will still want pleasure and there will be resentment for having to be good. Further, the superego will try to get us to conform to society's rules, but some rules will make no sense to a more practical ego. Why do I have to come to a full stop at a stop sign when no one is around? If I live in a deserted area, know the road, and it's sunny and quiet around, do I practically need to come to a full stop, or could I do a rolling stop? The superego sees a danger of not stopping completely, and the ego thinks it should lighten up. In this way the superego torments the "sinful" ego with anxiety and is on the lookout for opportunities to get it punished by the external world. This can create the strange phenomenon where the more virtuous a person is, the more this person may become distrustful and harsh toward their own motivations, desires, and actions "so that ultimately it is precisely those people who have carried saintliness furthest who reproach themselves with the worst sinfulness."[151] This is where self-knowledge and societal aid should, in a good society, ease the contradiction. We say that virtue is a reward in itself, but when one's self doesn't reward the self for being good, the internal "reward" doesn't trigger. Without a society and others helping you see your goodness, it's difficult to stay balanced. The person who is striving to be good but is unsure that he or she is, will suffer. Still, maturity also requires that we acknowledge that this contradiction is just part of what it means to be a moral person. It's tough, because some instincts that we must suppress to be good people just never go away. Consequently, they cause a somewhat constant frustration if not satisfied occasionally. We can say that good people feel the worst. The worst people don't feel.

Another intriguing aspect of the interplay between guilt, morality, and civilization involves the role of luck, or what Freud calls "ill-luck." In philosophy we call it "moral luck." When you don't suffer from your actions, you are less likely to feel guilty or to experience much pain and suffering. We all know of instances in our own life where we did things we should not have done but we never got in trouble. We either didn't get caught or the situation didn't escalate in a way it might have. Perhaps we drove recklessly but "got away with it." Having some luck in life makes life easier and, we might say, better. Not just because we are not in trouble with the external world and others but also from inside ourselves. For when we get punished from

---

[151] Ibid.

the outside world, our inner world remembers and tries to remind us and control us. Even thinking certain things, after having suffered from similar experiences, will make us ambivalent towards those very thoughts. Our conscience or superego will try to crush the thoughts before they become recurring actions. Even if the actions were not really bad or wrong, if we experienced pain or suffering from them, our superego will try to prevent us from doing the actions again. This leads to the bizarre result that some people are not punished externally or internally for bad behavior, because they got "lucky" — while other people will suffer from the inside and/or outside, for things not so bad, but simply because of "ill-luck." Similarly, within persons themselves, some innocuous things, because of ill luck, will stick with us, and other dangerous things — because of "luck" — will not bother us at all. Concerning the latter, we may continue to push the envelope recklessly in those dangerous things. We might have actually been luckier in the long run to have met with some trouble and been punished for it, when we were younger. This may have helped us curb certain behaviors. That's why society needs to be tough and help us grow into mature adults. Giving us excessive passes in life comes back to haunt all of us. Yes, this may appear to be unfair because no one determines good luck vs ill luck, but that's the point about reality that Freud is reminding us of: life is not metaphysically fair, just, or equal. We need to accept certain aspects of the world and the nature of human existence if we want to live according to true standards. Being driven by metaphysical notions of what's fair will result in ill-luck for oneself or for others.

We might think of "ill-luck" as merely a social construction, but as we saw above, it's a power and can quickly become a social force. Freud says not only individuals but whole groups of people will let themselves be directed by the phenomenon of luck. This is because the infantile stage of conscience is not gone with the appearance of the superego.[152] Fate is seen or felt as a substitute for the parental agency. Rather than face this uncomfortable truth, many today look to structures and simplified history to fill this void in their understanding and in their lack of power. Others in the social world may get behind the fashionable critiques so as to fit in. One should beware of fads, *non*? Those jumping on the bandwagon don't need to understand whether the critique is true and fair, so long as they can mimic the language. This infantile mimesis is a type of fragility that grants those willing to debase themselves "good luck" in society. Still, as with the people who secretly corrupt their minds online, they end up outfoxing themselves as they lose their only chance at having an ethical, free, and meaningful existence.

[152] Ibid., pp. 116-119.

In Freudian language, what is going on is that the threat of loss of love makes one bow to whatever "parental" representation his or her superego is standing in for. When the cultural superego loses its rationality and morality, it becomes what we called in the first chapter an unqualified authority. To maintain authoritative status, it must essentialize and demonize certain others. This works to distract from lack of competence and gives a story to bolster the lie. We see how easy it is to give in to weakness when we recognize that the work and energy of a being, evolving from pure id, to amoral follower of an authority, to a decent and rational human being, is really difficult even under the best of circumstances. There is always the temptation to just give in to the id or to an irrational cultural superego. Earlier historical ages used God to promote morality and grow individuality, but in our post-God society it's harder to find reasons to be good, and it's even more difficult to summon the motivation to strive for what's higher. Nonetheless, today, despite the lack of a rational and good cultural superego, most so-called ordinary people still want maturity, have a sense of the complexities of life, and see their personal roles in the fate of their lives. However, in narcissistic and opportunistic personalities, we witness a running right back to the id and a blaming of their lives on someone or something else. One with such a personality, when dealing with "misfortune...does not throw the blame on himself but on his fetish, which has obviously not done its duty, and he gives it a thrashing instead of punishing himself."[153] When these types hold the reins of our cultural superego, it threatens to put all of us back into an animal realm. The result of this type of thinking and acting is ill-luck for us all.

---

[153] Ibid., p. 119.

Conclusion: Still Discontent, Yet Forging

> Just as a planet revolves around a central body as well as rotating on its own axis, so the human individual takes part in the course of development of mankind at the same time as he pursues his own path in life.[154] —Sigmund Freud

In his final chapter,[155] Freud stresses that, unlike the process of civilization, the process of the individual aims directly for happiness. This is because of the power of the pleasure principle within us all. Still, for an individual to find happiness, "a human community appears as a scarcely avoidable condition which must be fulfilled before this aim of happiness can be achieved."[156] We need civilization and we have an urge, albeit weak, for it. Freud calls the urge for community "altruistic," and he adds that it can largely be satisfied simply "with the role of imposing restrictions."[157] The stronger urge in us, an "egoistic"[158] one, pursues individual happiness. Restricting ourselves is not sufficient to quench our egoistic thirst. We are agents and need to create in order to have true happiness. The French word for happiness, *bonheur*, implies having the good fortune to reach a state of savory sweetness. A piquant candy that is seemingly contradictory but, like the individual who has the good fortune to be born in the right civilization, comes into actualization thanks to lucky circumstances and a delightful inner self, somehow blending into a sublime French *bonbon*, so to speak. Ultimately it is derived from working on oneself, as in: *l'aboutissement d'une construction de*

---

[154] *Civilization and its Discontents*, p. 142.
[155] Ibid., Chapter Eight.
[156] Ibid., p. 141.
[157] Ibid.
[158] Ibid.

soi (the culmination of a building of the self). Still, as we have seen, the individual needs civilization to aid in this goal. If we could be happy without civilization, we might opt for that. We can't, and that's part of the reason why we are discontent. Civilization too, one might say, is discontent. Civilization needs individuals. At the same time it cannot tolerate individuals who are too individualistic. Therefore, civilization stresses the virtues of unity, harmony, self-sacrifice, community, and altruism. It attempts to make us simply part of its world. Thus, it cares little for individual happiness. Society won't waste time or energy on the individual's happiness unless forced to. Further, it has no problem seducing us into being satisfied with mere infantile desires. Satisfaction with shiny cultural objects and voguish social labels makes us easier to manage. If everybody is content eating designer cupcakes, why encourage them to read Chekhov? Does our world serve us cupcakes, or skills to contemplate Chekhov? Which is truly more readily available? Which is better for us? It's clear, we must push for more if we want to be more than a glaze for society, and if we want to evolve. True individuality requires capturing the "special features of its own which are not reproduced in the process of human civilization."[159]

Freud paints a powerful metaphoric picture of the complex phenomenon wherein each of us is an individual as well as being a component of society. He says that just as a planet revolves around a larger star while also rotating on its own axis, "so the human individual takes part in the course of development of mankind at the same time as he pursues his own path in life."[160] To the outside eye, the struggles and competing powers seem insignificant. In fact, the planets orbiting the star seem to spin and revolve effortlessly, harmoniously, and with necessity. However, if we look carefully, there is a vicious battle going on. Forces in the sky and on the earth constantly battle. Chaos often overpowers order. The conflicts are constant and ever changing. The two urges, for collective unity and individual happiness, fight within us all. Further, society will try to undercut one's individuality, while many individuals will not sacrifice for civilization. Fortunately, the fight between the individual and the society is not an eternal one of the magnitude of Eros and Thanatos. It's just a struggle "within the economics of the libido,"[161] very much like the struggle between ego and object instincts within us all. This gives us hope that our future can be better. It is up to individuals to seize their lives and artfully balance the energy and projects of both ego and object instincts. Further, we must come to terms with what type of civilization will

---

[159] Ibid., p. 142.
[160] Ibid.
[161] Ibid.

allow for both robust individual happiness and meaningful unity as a people. Are we mature enough for democracy? Are we emotionally intelligent and caring enough to live in a free society? Can we trust experts and those positioning for political power? Should philosophers be rulers?

Freud understands the struggles both within individuals and throughout societies. Our propensity for violence and domination is a formidable force that only can be countered with other material forces. Mere ideas (even fancy ones) and beliefs (even strong ones) will not be adequate to save us. As thinking beings, though, it's difficult for us to accept this. We want to believe in the power of our minds, principles, and theories. Freud says people "have at all times set the greatest value on ethics, as though they expected that it in particular would produce especially important results."[162] He adds that it is "the sorest spot in every civilization"[163] and it is therapeutic to attempt "to achieve, by means of a command of the super-ego, something which has so far not been achieved by means of any other cultural activities."[164] We must move beyond words and ideas and into the realm of individual and collective action before the sore spot turns into a glaring and ugly bruise. As Freud puts it, "a real change in the relations of human beings to possessions would be of more help in this direction than any ethical commands."[165]

Civilization is still packed with discontents. Modernity, in some ways, has just exacerbated our problems. A hermeneutic understanding of our condition would stress that we need to look honestly at the contexts in which we live our lives. We should attempt to live by the true standards that make the virtuous contexts virtuous. When we think of our life, we could aim to get the parts to fit with the whole. All the while, we could hold on to the understanding that this is impossible. A human life is complex, rich, and contradictory. Our lives will not fit together like a jigsaw puzzle. Rather our lives will consist of vicissitudes and periods of stability. With some luck we can win a championship or two in our lifetime. Still, most of the time on this planet, we could be useful, pursue excellence, and make our individual and collective lives valuable. We can evolve and can pursue meaningful commitments. We can have individual lives of meaning that connect to relevant and higher communities. However, each of us will have to face our own mortality one day and accept this fact with grace. In the meantime, let's forge ahead and make ourselves into something greater.

---

[162] Ibid., pp. 144.
[163] Ibid.
[164] Ibid.
[165] Ibid., p. 146.

C'est en forgeant qu'on devient forgeron

La vie philosophique doesn't throw out the baby with the bath water but rather helps the baby evolve into a full and complete human being. We live in a world after the death of God. Nonetheless, our world has remained thoroughly essentialist. Most people sense a version of the oceanic feeling and interpret it self-servingly. Philosophically speaking, many people, still today, have a metaphysical urge. Many individuals also have an anti-metaphysical urge. Finally, there might be a growing attitude in many people of what we might call an un-metaphysical comportment. In other words, an indifference or boredom in anything of substance, an apathy or lack of curiosity in both transcendence and individual evolution. For the latter, the market can keep producing sugary pacifiers. Meanwhile, places and spaces that encourage and reward nobility and worthwhile duty are scarce. At the same time the "freedom" to avoid duty and bypass nobility has not ushered in happiness or true freedom. It has simply muddied the world and dirtied those living in it. Some things do seem clear. Today essentialist thinking has attached itself to various identities. Much of civilization is unhealthy; many individuals suffer existential angst, have an air of malaise, and remain discontent. Most solutions presented to us today are lacking in hermeneutic coherence, virtuous comportment, and true standards. This creates an ideological world that preaches unhelpful clichés such as practice makes perfect or, even more absurdly, perfect practice makes perfect. Neither is true and the ones selling the lies are art forgers. Still, our deeper and richest traditions know this and teach us how to stay on the true path and how to avoid the imitators.

"Our life is a warfare, and a mere pilgrimage. Fame after life is no better than oblivion. What is it then that will adhere and follow?"[166] What then can guide those who have turned their backs on the false standards? What path can we take toward true happiness? Our tradition tells us the path is philosophy. For Marcus Aurelius and Plato, it is the practice of *la vie philosophique*. "And philosophy doth consist in this, for a man to preserve that spirit which is within him, from all manner of contumelies and injuries, and above all pains or pleasures; never to do anything either rashly, or feignedly, or hypocritically: wholly to depend from himself and his own proper actions."[167] "It is always the case, though, whenever anyone arrives at the life here [on earth], that if he engages in philosophy in a healthy way and the lot for his choice doesn't fall among the last ones, he stands a good chance, based on the reports from the other place, not only being happy here but also that his

---

[166] Marcus Aurelius, *Meditations*. Book Two, XV, Project Gutenberg, https://www.gutenberg.org/files/2680/2680-h/2680-h.htm#link2H_4_0019.
[167] Marcus Aurelius, *Meditations*, Book Two, XV.

journey from here to there and back again will not be traveled underground on a rough road but on a smooth one through the heavens."[168] These philosophers uttered those words thousands of years ago. They saw the potential in us. They were optimistic about humanity. They understood that *philosophia* is not wisdom but the love of wisdom. *C'est en pratiquant la vie philosophique qu'on devient sage.* We can become sage-like. As agents we must acknowledge that the philosophical life is a choice. It must be chosen and practiced daily. We either live *la vie philosophique* or we don't. There are no shortcuts to acquire true happiness. There are many wrong paths, paths that lead to nowhere, journeys that fail us. There is a true path. Ergo, why not be brave? Why not say "*non*" to the false standards? Why not give the practice of the philosophical life an honest effort?

Plato promised that "we might be friends to ourselves and to the gods, both while we remain here in this place and when we carry off the rewards for it like athletes on their victory laps. Both here and in the thousand-year journey we've been going through, we will do well."[169] Our gods are the true standards. They guide us in becoming true friends to ourselves, to others, and to our world. They tell us that to live well in one's environment, we must understand our qualities and capabilities, we must act with virtuosity, while carrying the proper weapons and tools that allow us to be truly connected to others who matter.

We must forge. *C'est en forgeant qu'on devient forgeron.* This French saying is not essentialist. It's concrete and contextual but also connects with lived history and higher practices. It's by working with a forge that we become blacksmiths. We become blacksmiths not by talking about it or reading about it or wishing for it. It's not a linguistic miracle. We must practice in the right community for a long time. We must see and mimic others making virtuous artifacts and working on higher things with others. We must also understand our qualities and aptitudes. The training, the trial and error, the history of the craft, and the community are necessary conditions for virtuosity. We must train our bodies and work our minds while reflecting on various options. Ultimately, we must choose the higher ground and the greater good. It takes physical practice, contextual intelligence, time, object-understanding, and the ego-strength to persevere. We will fail many times before we get it right. Excellence and greatness do not happen overnight or on the first try. True happiness is not fabricated nor is it found outside a noble civilization.

---

[168] Plato, *Republic* (Hackett, 2007), p. 320-321.
[169] *Republic*, p. 322.

BIBLIOGRAPHY

Adorno, Theodor. *Aesthetic Theory*. Robert Hullot-Kentor, trans. Minneapolis. Minnesota Press. 1997.

_____. *Minima Moralia*. E. F. N. Jephcott, trans. London. Verso. 1994.

_____. *Negative Dialectics*. E. B. Ashton, trans. New York. Continuum. 1992.

Arato, Andrew. "Lukács's Theory of Reification." *Telos* 11. Spring 1972.

Arato, Andrew and Paul Breines. *The Young Lukács and the Origins of Western Marxism*. New York. Seabury Press. 1979.

Aristotle. *The Basic Works of Aristotle*. New York. Random House. 1941.

Aurelius, Marcus. *Meditations*. Book Two, XV, Project Gutenberg, https://www.gutenberg.org/files/2680/2680-h/2680-h.htm#link2H_4_0019.

Badiou, Alain. *Theory of the Subject*, Bruno Bostells, trans. London. Continuum. 2009.

Baudelaire, Charles. *Flowers of Evil*. New York. Dover. 1992.

Berman, Marshall. *Adventures in Marxism*. London. Verso. 1999.

Bernstein, J. M. "Lukács Wake: Praxis, Presence, and Metaphysics." *Lukács Today*. Rockmore. 1988.

Bull, Malcolm. *Anti-Nietzsche*. Verso. 2019.

Camus, Albert. *The Myth of Sisyphus*. Knopf Doubleday Publishing. 2018.

Carroll, Sean. *The Big Picture*. Dutton. 2016.

Chaucer, Geoffrey. *The Canterbury Tales*. Insignia Publishing. 2016.

Cohen, Jean, L. and Andrew Arato. *Civil Society and Political Theory*. Cambridge. The MIT Press. 1992.

Derrida, Jacques. *Of Grammatology*. John Hopkins University Press. 2016.

_____. *Margins of Philosophy*. University of Chicago Press. 1985.

_____. *Writing and Difference*. University of Chicago Press. 2017.

Descartes, *Discourse on Method*. Penguin Classics. 2000.

_____. *Meditations on First Philosophy*. Donald A. Cress, trans. Indianapolis. Hackett Publishing.1993.

Donovan, Thomas. *Dialectic of Enlightenment as Sport*. New York. Algora. 2015.

_____. *The False Dialectic Between Christians and Atheists*, New York. Algora. 2016.

Eagleton, Terry. *Culture and the Death of God*. New Haven. Yale University Press. 2014.

_____. *Ideology*. New York. Verso. 1991.

_____. *On Evil*. New Haven. Yale University Press. 2010.

_____. *Reason, Faith, and Revolution*. New Haven. Yale University Press. 2009.

Epictetus. *Enchiridion*. Dover Thrift Editions. 2004.

Epicurus. *The Epicurus Reader*. Hackett Publishing. 1994.

Feenberg. Andrew. *Lukács, Marx and the Sources of Critical Theory*. Oxford. Martin Robertson. 1981.

Feuerbach, Ludwig. *The Essence of Christianity*. George Eliot, trans. New York. Prometheus Books. 1989.

Foucault, Michel. *Discipline and Punish*. Alan Sheridan, trans. New York. Vintage Books. 1977.

Freud, Sigmund. *Civilization and Its Discontents*. New York. W. W. Norton. 1989.

_____. *The Future of an Illusion*. New York. W. W. Norton. 1989.

_____. *The Interpretation of Dreams*. Basic Books. 2010.

_____. *The Essays on the Theory of Sexuality*. Verso. 2017.

_____. *Totem and Taboo*, Project Gutenberg, Retrieved May 15, 2023. https://www.gutenberg.org/files/41214/41214-h/41214-h.htm.

Fukuyama, Francis. *America at the Crossroads*. New Haven. Yale University Press. 2006.

_____. *The End of History and the Last Man*. New York. Free Press. 2006.

Gadamer, Hans-Georg. *Truth and Method*. Continuum. New York. 1996.

Guess, Raymond. *Changing the Subject: Philosophy from Socrates to Adorno*. Harvard University Press. 2017.

_____. *Not Thinking Like a Liberal*. Belknap Press. 2022.

_____. *Who Needs a World View?* Harvard Press. 2020.

Habermas, Jürgen. *Between Facts and Norms*. William Rehg, trans. Cambridge. MIT Press. 1996.

_____. *Between Naturalism and Religion*. Cambridge. Polity Press. 2008.

_____. *Postmetaphysical Thinking II*. Polity. 2017.

_____. Habermas and Joseph Ratzinger. *The Dialectics of Secularization*. San Francisco. Ignatius Press. 2005.

_____. *The Theory of Communicative Action*. Beacon Press. 1981.

Hadot, Pierre. *The Inner Citadel*. Harvard University Press. 1998.

_____. *What is Ancient Philosophy?* Harvard University Press. 2002.

Hall, Stuart. *Modernity*. Cambridge. Blackwell. 1996.

Harvey, David. *The Condition of Postmodernity*. Cambridge. Blackwell Press. 1990.

_____. *The Limits To Capital*. New York. Verso. 1999.

Hawking, Stephen. *The Grand Design*. New York. Bantam Books. 2010.

Hegel, G. W. F., *Elements of the Philosophy of Right*. H. B. Nisbet, trans. Cambridge. Cambridge University Press. 1991.

_____. *The Encyclopaedia Logic*. Indianapolis. Hackett Publishing. 1991.

_____. *Phenomenology of Spirit*. A. V. Miller, trans. Oxford. Oxford University Press. 1977.

Heidegger, Martin. *Basic Writing*. Harper Perennial Modern Classics. 2008

_____. *Being and Time*. San Francisco. HarperSan Francisco 1962.

_____. *The Question Concerning Technology, and Other Essays*. Harper Perennial Modern Classics. 2013.

_____. *Poetry, Language, Thought*. Harper Perennial Modern Classics. 2013.

Homer. *Iliad*. Stanley Lombardo, trans. Cambridge. Hackett Publishing. 1997.

_____. *Odyssey*. Stanley Lombardo, trans. Cambridge. Hackett Publishing. 2000.

Honneth, Axel. *Reification*. New York. Oxford. 2008.

Horkheimer, Max and Theodor W. Adorno. *Dialectic of Enlightenment*. Edmund Jephcott, trans. Stanford. Stanford University Press. 2002.

Horkheimer, Max. *Eclipse of Reason*. London. Continuum. 2004.

Jameson, Fredric. *Marxism and Form*. New Jersey. Princeton University Press. 1971.

_____. *The Political Unconscious*. New York. Cornell University Press. 1981.

Jay, Martin. *Adorno*. Cambridge. Harvard University Press. 1984.

_____. "Habermas and Modernism," in *Habermas and Modernity*, ed. Richard J. Bernstein. Cambridge. MIT Press. 1991.

_____. *Marxism and Totality*. Berkeley. University of California Press. 1984.

Kant, Immanuel. *Critique of Practical Reason*. Cambridge Press. 2015.

_____. *Critique of Pure Reason*. Norman Kemp Smith, trans. New York. St. Martin's Press. 1965.

_____. *Groundwork of the Metaphysics of Morals*. Cambridge Press. 2012.

Kaufmann, Walter. "Freud and the Tragic Virtues," in The American Scholar Vol. 29 No. 4 August 1960.

Kellner, Douglas. *Critical Theory, Marxism and Modernity*. Baltimore. John Hopkins University Press. 1989.

Kierkegaard, Soren. *Fear and Trembling*. London. Oxford University Press. 1939.

King James Bible. Genesis. The Project Gutenberg. May 1, 2023.

Kirk, Raven, Schofield. *The Presocratic Philosophers: A Critical History with a Selection of Texts.* Cambridge Publishing. 1984.

Kundera, Molan. *The Art of the Novel.* Linda Asher, trans. New York. HarperCollins. 2000.

_____. *The Festival of Insignificance.* Linda Asher, trans. New York. Harper. 2015.

_____. *Ignorance.* Linda Asher, trans. New York. Perennial. 2002.

_____. *Immortality.* Peter Kussi, trans. New York. HarperPerennial. 1991.

_____. *Slowness.* Linda Asher, trans. New York. Harper. 1996.

_____. *The Unbearable Lightness of Being.* Michael Henry Heim, trans. New York. Harper. 1984.

Lacan, Jacques. *Autres écrits.* Éditions du Seuil. 2001.

_____. *Écrits.* Éditions du Seuil. 1966.

Lahiri, Jhumpa. *In Other Words.* Ann Goldstein, trans. New York. Knopf. 2016.

_____. *Whereabouts.* New York, Knopf. 2021.

Lefebvre, Henri. *Critique of Everyday Life.* John Moore, trans. New York. Verso. 1991.

Lotz, Christian. *The Capitalist Schema.* Lexington Press. 2016.

Lucretius. *On the Nature of Things.* Hackett Publishing. 2001.

Lukács, Georg. *A Defense of History and Class Consciousness.* Esther Leslie, trans. London. Verso. 2000.

_____. *History and Class Consciousness.* Rodney Livingstone, trans. Cambridge. MIT Press. 1971.

_____. *Marxism and Human Liberation.* New York. Dell Publishing, 1973.

_____. *The Ontology of Social Being.* (Hegel, Marx, Labour). Merlin Press. 1978.

_____. *Soul and Form.* Anna Bostock, trans. Cambridge. The MIT Press. 1971.

_____. *The Theory of the Novel.* Anna Bostock, trans. Cambridge. MIT Press. 1999.

_____. *Writer and Critic,* London. Merlin Press. 1978.

Marcuse, Herbert. *Eros and Civilization.* Boston. Beacon Press. 1966.

_____. *One-Dimensional Man.* Boston. Beacon Press. 1964.

_____. *Reason and Revolution: Hegel and the Rise of Social Theory.* Boston. 1960.

Marx, Karl. *Capital* vol. one. Ben Fowkes, trans. New York. Vintage Books. 1977.

Marx, Karl and Frederick Engels. *The Communist Manifesto.* Samuel Moore, trans. New York. Washington Square Press. 1964.

Marx. *Economic and Philosophic Manuscripts of 1844.* New York. Prometheus. 1988.

_____. *The Marx-Engels Reader.* New York. W. W. Norton. 1978.

Molière. *Le Bourgeois gentilhomme.* Les éditions Bordas. 1993.

_____. *Les Précieuses ridicules.* Les éditions Bordas. 1967.

Nehamas, Alexander. *Nietzsche: Life as Literature.* Cambridge. Harvard University Press. 1985.

_____. "Nietzsche, modernity, aestheticism." Bernd Magnus and Kathleen M. Higgins, *The Cambridge Companion to Nietzsche.* Cambridge. Cambridge University Press. 1996.

Nietzsche, Frederick. *Beyond Good and Evil.* Vintage Press. 1989.

_____. *The Portable Nietzsche.* Walter Kaufmann, trans. New York. Penguin Books. 1982.

_____. *Twilight of the Idols and The Anti-Christ.* R. J. Hollingdale, trans. London. Penguin Publishing. 2003.

Ollman, Bertell, *Alienation.* Cambridge. Cambridge University Press. 1976.

Onfray, Michel. *Atheist Manifesto.* Jeremy Leggatt, trans. New York. Arcade Publishing. 2007.

Palmer, Donald. *Does the Center Hold?* McGraw Hill. 2014.

Pamuk, Zeynep. *Politics and Expertise: How to use Science in a Democratic Society.* Princeton University Press. 2021.

Pascal, Blaise. *Pensées.* Project Gutenberg. April, 2023.

Perry, Louise. *The Case Against the Sexual Revolution.* Polity Press. 2022.

Plato. *Phaedo,* Oxford. 2009.

_____.*Republic.* Hackett Publishing. 2007.

_____. *Symposium.* Hackett Publishing. 1989.

_____. *Symposium.* Project Gutenberg. April 2023.

_____. *The Trial and Death of Socrates.* Indianapolis. Hackett Publishing. 2000.

Ricoeur, Paul. *The Conflict of Interpretations.* Northwestern University Press. 2007.

_____. *Freud & Philosophy: An Essay on Interpretation.* New Haven, Yale University Press. 1970.

Rorty, Richard. *Contingency, Irony, and Solidarity.* Cambridge. Cambridge University Press. 1989.

_____. *Take Care of Freedom and Truth Will Take Care of Itself.* Stanford. Stanford Press. 2005.

Roy, Olivier, *Holy Ignorance.* New York. Columbia University Press. 2010.

Sartre, Jean-Paul. *Being and Nothingness.* Washington Square Press. 2021.

_____. *Existentialism and Human Emotions.* New York. Citadel Press. 1985.

_____. *Nausea.* New Directions Press. 2013.

Schiller, Friedrick. Kallias Letters (1793). The Schiller Institute. https://archive.schillerinstitute.com/transl/trans_schil_essay.html.

Schopenhauer, Arthur. *The World as Will and Representation.* E. F. J. Payne, trans. New York. Dover Publications. 1969.

Schwitzgebel, Eric. "In-between believing," *Philosophical Quarterly* 51: 76–82. 2001.

Stern, Alex. "Critical Theory and the Newest Left." *Hedgehog Review.* 6/25/2021.

_____. *The Fall of Language: Benjamin and Wittgenstein on Meaning.* Harvard University Press. 2019.

Taylor, Charles, *Hegel*. Cambridge. Cambridge University Press. 1975.

Vogel, Steven. *Against Nature*. Albany. State University of New York Press. 1996.

_____. "Marx and Alienation from Nature." *Social Theory and Practice*, Vol. 14, No. 3, Fall 1988.

_____. *Thinking like a Mall*. Cambridge. The MIT Press. 2015.

Voltaire. *Candide*. Bordas. 1984.

_____. *Candide*. The Project Gutenberg. eBook, Boni & Liveright, Inc. 1918.

Warnke, Georgia. *After Identity*. Cambridge Press. 2008.

_____. *Debating Sex and Gender*. Oxford Press. 2010.

_____. *Gadamer*. Stanford. Stanford University Press. 1987.

_____. *Legitimate Differences: Interpretation in the Abortion Controversy and Other Public Debates*. Berkeley. University of California Press. 1999.

_____. "We Need a More Context Sensitive Conception of Identity." *Areo Magazine*. 7/12/2020.

Wiggershaus, Rolf. *The Frankfurt School*. Michael Robertson, trans. Cambridge. The MIT Press. 1994.

Žižek, Slavoj. *How to Read Lacan*. Norton Publishing. 2007.

_____. *Less Than Nothing*. London. Verso. 2012.

_____. *The Puppet and the Dwarf*. Cambridge. The MIT Press. 2003.

_____. *The Sublime Object of Ideology*. London. Verso. 1999.

INDEX OF NAMES

Printed in the United States
by Baker & Taylor Publisher Services